Everybody Has a Podcast

(except you)

Also by the McElroys

BY CLINT MCELROY, GRIFFIN MCELROY, JUSTIN MCELROY, AND TRAVIS MCELROY

The Adventure Zone: Petals to the Metal

The Adventure Zone: Murder on the Rockport Limited!

The Adventure Zone: Here There Be Gerblins

BY JUSTIN MCELROY AND SYDNEE MCELROY

The Sawbones Book: The Hilarious, Horrifying Road to Modern Medicine

Everybody Has a Podcast

(except you)

A How-to Guide from the
First Family of Podcasting

**Justin McElroy,
Travis McElroy,
and
Griffin McElroy**

HARPER ● PERENNIAL

NEW YORK ● LONDON ● TORONTO ● SYDNEY ● NEW DELHI ● AUCKLAND

HARPER ● PERENNIAL

Contributions to the "Research" section of chapter one, "Preproduction," provided by Sydnee McElroy, with Teresa McElroy and Rachel McElroy.

Headshot illustrations by Sarah McKay.

HarperCollins books may be purchased for educational, business, or sales promotional use. For information, please email the Special Markets Department at SPsales@harpercollins.com.

FIRST EDITION

Designed by Jen Overstreet

Library of Congress Cataloging-in-Publication Data has been applied for.

ISBN 978-0-06-297480-8

21 22 23 24 25   LSC   10 9 8 7 6 5 4 3 2

To Mom and Dad, who taught us that we could be anything when we grew up. Sorry it wasn't scientists or lawyers.

Contents

Introduction • ix

Chapter One: Preproduction • • • • • • • • • • • 1

Chapter Two: Tools • • • • • • • • • • • • • • • • • 57

Chapter Three: Let's Record • • • • • • • • • • • • 99

Chapter Four: Now Let's Make It Listenable • • • 125

Chapter Five: Please, Someone, Anyone: Listen • • 157

Chapter Six: Making Money • • • • • • • • • • • 199

Outroduction • • • • • • • • • • • • • • • • • • 231

You Honestly Want More McElroy Content? • • • 237

Acknowledgments • • • • • • • • • • • • • • • • 239

Index • 241

Introduction
with Justin McElroy

As much as it pains us to admit it, podcasting is easy.

You buy a mic and talk into it and record that talking and then publish it. It's easy!

It must be easy, or we, the McElroy brothers, wouldn't have been successful at it. We've had #1 podcasts in the health, gaming, and comedy categories, and we're three-time #1 *New York Times* bestselling authors. We tour around the country recording our podcasts in front of sold-out crowds. Most inspirationally of all, we've done it all with what would charitably be described as "the median amount of natural talent."

Don't believe me? Okay, let's meet the McElroy brothers real quick:

Justin (the Oldest)

Once got fired from Blockbuster Video for stealing a copy of *Fight Club* that had been set aside for the store's owner to purchase.

Travis (the Middlest)

Spent his high school years wearing exclusively button-up shirts and tear-away pants.

Griffin (the Youngest)

Once went viral for eating a banana with the peel on.

Reader, our dad, Clint, once knocked himself unconscious by accidentally dumping bleach onto kitty litter.

We're not the cream of the crop, is what we're saying.

Sure, we've glommed on to the actual, tangible talents of our wives, family, and friends who've helped us launch a lot of our most successful shows. You could accuse us of bringing in more entertaining ringers and you wouldn't be wrong. But our oldest podcast, *My Brother, My Brother and Me,* is just us three goobers passing out bad advice. We've been doing it for more than a decade and a lot of people listen, believe it or not.

So, yes, scientifically speaking, podcasting is easy. So, why do you need a book about it? Well, it may be easy, but you can still do it wrong. Trust us on this, we've been screwing up for more than ten years now, in ways small and massive. We're still screwing up. We'll probably screw up today.

Podcasting, at least when you're doing it well, comprises a staggering number of different disciplines. You have to be a host, an organizer, an editor, a marketer, and probably a few other positions we're forgetting. While podcasting isn't difficult, there is . . . a lot of it.

Before you panic, take heart! When taken one at a time, none of the skills that compose good podcasting is particularly difficult to attain. (Again, *we* did it.) So that's what we're going to do. We're going to take our decade of podcasting experience and break it into clear, nonfussy, nontechnical chunks that anyone can absorb and use to make a podcast they can be proud of.

First, we're going to help you come up with a show topic and structure. We'll advise you on how to pick your cohosts, art, and music for your show and some basic recording techniques. We'll talk you through buying equipment, which won't be as expensive as you're imagining, we promise.

Next, it's the technical info: the editing, the postproduction, finding a place to host the file. All the nerdlinger stuff we promise is a lot less excruciatingly boring than it sounds.

With your show on its feet, we'll focus on growing your audience and interacting with listeners. (Short version: Act like a decent human being.) If you want to get really ambitious, we can even talk through ways to make a few bucks off your podcast, like with ad sales, listener support, and selling merchandise.

Finally, we'll explain how to take all that we've taught you and spend a decade honing your craft, then write a book containing all your knowledge. Only then, once the cycle begins anew, will we be allowed to die and ascend to heaven.

We . . . should have left that last part out.

Hey, who's ready to start podcasting?

Everybody Has a Podcast

(except you)

CHAPTER ONE
Preproduction

What's Your Podcast About?

WITH JUSTIN MCELROY

In podcasting's golden era (or at least when we started our first show in 2010), you didn't need your podcast to really be about anything. Hell, you barely even needed a microphone. There were fewer podcasts in those days, and listeners were just happy to have something, anything, to fill the terrible silence.

That's not just me pining for a simpler time, though I'm thirty-nine now, so I do that a lot. But it's important for you to understand that your favorite show, especially if it's been around for a while, is probably not a good model for what a podcast can be about.

As of this writing there are something like 850,000 podcasts out there according to Podcast Insights. You might be the world's most charming conversationalist or gifted storyteller, but unless you're already a big star, you aren't going to rise above the din without a great concept. You just won't. There are just too many podcasts competing for the same oxygen. Ear . . . oxygen. You get the idea.

First, you need your concept. You can start with a paragraph about what you want to achieve and how exactly you'll go about it, but it's important to be able to boil it down to a single-sentence pitch. Remember, the pitch isn't just for you. You want your audience to be able to spread the word about your show in a way that is both concise and interesting. Can you sell it in a sentence? That's your pitch.

Heck, even the big stars have more success when they have a strong pitch. The first line of the Apple Podcasts listing for *Anna Faris Is Unqualified* is "Not-great-relationship advice from completely unqualified Hollywood types." There's your pitch right there (and it's a good one).

The Big Sentence

You may be tempted to start with that one-sentence pitch, but it's putting the podcast cart before the podcast horse (his name is Bucko, by the way, and he's a delight). Instead, let's use that one sentence as a navigational star to guide us through this process. Give yourself the freedom to roam around as you hone your pitch. But if you find you can no longer boil your pitch down to one punchy sentence, you'll know you've gone astray.

If we were launching *My Brother, My Brother and Me* today . . . well, we wouldn't. Or at least we wouldn't in its current state. Let's try to pitch it.

"Three brothers give bad advice, but it's funny."

It's short! That's good! But it falls apart in the last two words: "it's funny." The listener hears our pitch and rightly replies, "Who says it's funny?" We look at one another furtively and blurt out, "Uh, we do?" Except we're talking to nobody because the listener has already moved on to one of the other half million shows.

Let's look at one of our much more recent shows: *The McElroy Brothers Will Be in "Trolls 2."* I'd write the pitch out for you, but the title really says it (more on that later). Three non-celebrities try to con their way into a major motion picture. Now, maybe that's a show for you, maybe it's not, but you're at least able to make an instant judgment call about whether you want to listen. My show *Sawbones: A Marital Tour of Misguided Medicine* is . . . well, it's right there in the subtitle, isn't it?

So, that's the big sentence, let's start building it.

Why Are You Here?

Why do you want to make a podcast? Do you want fame and fortune? Do you want to spread awareness of something? Do you want to contribute to a community? Do you want an excuse to talk with friends? They're all completely valid reasons to start a podcast, but they will each shape your show differently.

Justin just kinda casually granted you fame and fortune, but let me do a little expectation setting. Podcasting is a long game. I know podcasts that didn't start getting real attention until they had already produced more than one hundred episodes. Most people don't start listening to a show until they can binge at least ten episodes. If your show releases biweekly, that's five months of work before you see any noticeable audience growth. It took us more than eight years of podcasting before we were able to all make it our full-time jobs. What I'm saying is making money is great, but you are probably going to be making your show for free for a while. Maybe for as long as the show exists.

Let's say you have a great time talking about old movies with your friends and you think, "This is hysterical, we should be recording this!" That's . . . well, it's an extremely twenty-first-century impulse, isn't it? Regardless, it's not a bad seed for a podcast. But there are an unfathomable number of shows in that vein. *Doug Loves Movies, The Flop House, How Did This Get Made?* . . . we could go on. It's dizzying. If it's the show you wanna make, go for it! But keep in mind that unless you have an incredibly smart hook, it's gonna be *real* tough to grow a large audience and stand out from the crowd.

On the flip side, maybe your goal is just to make a massively successful podcast, so you research current trends and analyze the stats and find that "profiles of artisanal yak shavers" is the next big thing. You pay thousands for your promotional art, you book Malcolm Gladwell for your first episode, and then you realize something: you fucking hate yaks. Can't stand talking about the things. You may have positioned your show for success, but you don't care about the topic, which is a recipe for disaster in terms of both building an audience and your personal happiness.

If you wanna make a show that's just for you and your friends to goof around with, I think that's great and cool and worthwhile. There are probably large swaths of this book you can skip if you want. That's fine, you bought the book, do what you want with it. As an independent podcaster, you have the benefit of not having to worry about being canceled by a studio. So you might have an audience of only twenty, but if those twenty people really love your show and you really love making it, who cares? If you've made something that brings joy to yourself and to others, even if it's only a few people, you're a success.

If audience size isn't your priority, make peace with that now. If you can free yourself from the burden of worrying about how many people are listening, you're going to save yourself a lot of stress down the line.

Even though I'm not opposed to the idea of vanity podcasting, for lack of a better term, I would humbly urge you to take a moment and consider if there's a way you could make your movie chat show something lots of people would want to listen to. You're putting in the work to inject something into the world—why not try to make it something the world might want?

Whether the show is designed for an audience of one or an audience of millions, there is one constant: it's not worth making a podcast you don't really care about. Audiences are savvy and podcasting is an intimate medium; they're gonna spot someone feigning enthusiasm for yaks a mile away and they're going to turn the podcast off every single time.

What Do You Obsess About?

If I were to ask you what you cared about, your answer would likely be fairly instinctual. My family. My job. The planet. That's good! You're a human being with your priorities well in order.

But I want to know what you obsess about. What headlines are you irresistibly compelled to click on when they pop up on your timeline? What do you find your fingers googling before your brain realizes what's happening? What do you passionately explain to friends and family despite the fact that they couldn't give a solitary shit? That's where your podcast needs to live.

You know something I'm obsessed with? Workplace training videos. I think the first one I saw was made in the mid-1980s and it was called "Wendy's Grill Skills." In it, a magical, digital ghost pulls a young man into a TV screen and then raps at him while detailing proper burger-frying technique. How could I not be hooked?

I could talk about workplace training videos endlessly. I show them to friends and family who always reward me with expressions of bemusement. If I could talk to the people who made these weird little examples of non-entertainment, I'd be in heaven. I'm utterly fascinated by them.

My other obsession is cereal, and I already make that podcast. It's a meditative show about cereal called *The Empty Bowl* that I host with a cereal blogger named Dan Goubert. I don't profit off it, and it has a much smaller audience than many of our other shows, but people have told me that it helps them to relax in trying times, and I get to talk about stuff I love, so it's a success.

Do you have a weird little part of your brain that you devote to that kind of minutiae? I think it's time you jam a metaphorical microphone up there and make that bit of think meat earn its keep by selling underwear and mattresses to eager listeners. The beauty of living in the internet age is that you don't have to find a local audience! If .0002 percent of the world population is interested in your topic, you have an audience of 15,600 people! If you need more convincing, look at how many vibrant subreddits and forums there are devoted to obsessively discussing a facet of a sliver of a tiny nugget of pop culture. There's one called, I kid you not, PicturesOfIanSleeping that is just pictures of some guy named Ian sleeping. It's got more than forty-four thousand followers. It takes all kinds, folks.

You notice I didn't say I'm obsessed with YouTube (where most of these videos live) or workplaces in general. I'd argue that those are too broad to justify an obsession. The cool thing about how fragmented the internet is is that you can find success without trying to cover huge topics on a very surface level. If you dive deep into a specific niche, you'll likely find some willing souls to follow you down. Don't be *Entertainment Tonight*, be *Self-Produced Beanie Baby–Collecting Tips Videos Tonight*.

Who Else Is Here?

Once you have an idea for the topic you want to cover, you'll want to know how it's already been done. (And it probably has,

I'm sorry to say. Did I mention there are a lot of podcasts?) So, let's research the competition.

Competition, by the way, is useful shorthand here, but it isn't a very useful way of thinking about this. If you're putting the work into coming up with a creative, smart approach to your subject, your show will be an entity unto itself. Just because someone already listens to a *Survivor* recap show, it doesn't mean they can't make room in their heart for yours.

According to a 2019 report from Edison Research, 32 percent of Americans listen to podcasts on a monthly basis. The way I see it, any podcast that makes a big impact and brings new people into the ecosystem is a boon for everyone who makes podcasts.

Let's stick with *Survivor*. Search the various podcasting directories like Apple Podcasts or Stitcher for *Survivor* and see what's out there. How are other people talking about *Survivor*? What's working (and not working) about that approach? For example, the *"Survivor" Fans Podcast* is a recap that features audio from other viewers of the show. *Rob Has a Podcast* is hosted by a former contestant (there are more than a few of those). *The "Survivor" Historians Podcast* is about the highlights of the show's past.

The *Survivor* market has been well saturated, but so has pretty much any popular TV show. You may decide that there are too many *Survivor* podcasts out there to rise above the noise. That might be true, and you may want to explore some other obsessions. Either way, you'll be making an informed decision and won't risk launching a replica of a show that already has a legion of fans and a feature film adaptation in the pipeline.

A Way In

Whether you're dealing with a topic that's been done to death or never been touched, where you'll absolutely need to differentiate yourself is how you approach the subject you want to work in. The more specific you can make your angle, the better. When our friends Tim Batt and Guy Montgomery came up with *The Worst Idea of All Time*, they didn't make "a podcast about *Grown Ups 2*." They watched and reviewed *Grown Ups 2* every week for a year. *99% Invisible* isn't just a show about design; it's the remarkable stories of how unremarkable things came to exist in the world.

Competitive research is a good jumping-off point. Now that you know about the *Survivor* shows that do exist, you can find the facet of *Survivor* you are obsessed with that nobody else is talking about. Interested in how the strategic metagame has evolved over time? There's probably a show there. Do you and your friends like predicting how it will all shake out? Maybe a *Survivor* fantasy draft would be a fun way to go.

If you've got a specific expertise in your topic, you should try to build an approach around it. My wife, Sydnee McElroy, is a physician, so we didn't do a generic podcast about history, we did one about the evolution of medicine throughout the years and how it's applied today. Sydnee's expertise is the central strength of *Sawbones*, and it would have been silly not to take advantage of it.

If the topic you want to discuss is more general, or you want to talk about a lot of different issues, you can set yourself apart by switching up the lens through which you view these issues. For example, Travis and his friends Brent Black and Courtney Enlow technically did a news show, but *Trends Like These* let social media popularity be the metric for what deserved discussion.

Anytime you think you might have your angle, ask yourself two questions:

1. Do I actually want to put in the time, my most precious resource on this planet, to make this thing exist on Earth?
2. Did I wish I didn't have to put in the work to make it exist, because I would adore being able to just listen to it?

If you've got a "yes" to both of those questions, you're ready to pick a name.

The Simple Guide to Picking a Great Name

I honestly have no fucking clue. Nobody does. Anybody who says differently is lying. I don't even know if this is the point at which you should pick a name. You could probably wait. I am pulling this out of my ass.

> Sometimes I think of a funny name for a podcast and then build the show around it. For example, *Positiviteeny!* was such a fun name that I couldn't help but develop it into a show. However, I do not recommend this way of going about it, because you will keep thinking of fun names and end up doing eighteen podcasts.

Okay, okay, I can maybe give you a few general guidelines, but then you're on your own.

- **Shorter is probably better.** It's easier to remember, easier to search for, easier to put on a T-shirt.
- **Don't put your name in it unless people know who you are.** If I don't recognize the name, I assume it's not a show for me.
- **Maybe it's a manifesto.** *Guys We F****d* communicates a staggering amount in three words: it's funny, it's for adults, it's irreverent, it's a show at least partially about sex.
- **Maybe it's not.** *Stop Podcasting Yourself* doesn't actually de-

scribe the show itself, but the silly intelligence of it communicates a lot about the show thematically.

- **Maybe it's bad.** *My Brother, My Brother and Me* doesn't mean anything and it's not evocative of our show. But we figured it out. Who knows?

I've got one more guideline that I'm gonna break out of the list because it's so important:

Make sure it's original.

Ideally, you're the only media source to use this name. There's a Wild West mystery book called *Sawbones* with eighty-eight reviews on Amazon, and it still screws up my Google Alerts weekly. At the very least you absolutely want to be the only podcast with the name. The last thing you want is to have to explain to everyone alive that you're "the other *This American Life*."

If you're torn between a few names, you should check if the name, or some simple take on it, is available on social media. We were very lucky to get @Sawbones. It makes sharing that handle so easy. @TheZoneCast sucks. Who can ever remember that?

The important thing really is that you know what you're in for so you can plan for it. I once launched a podcast called *The Besties* without the knowledge that the now-defunct Whiskey Media made a video series of the same name. I learned that bit of trivia roughly seventeen nanoseconds after my show launched, though, from approximately seventeen thousand angry tweets that cascaded upon me like the Red Sea if Moses had gotten distracted halfway through the crossing.

The Short Version
- Pick what you want to talk about.
- See who else is talking about it.
- Figure out how you want to talk about it.

Cohosts: Should You Have One?

WITH TRAVIS MCELROY

One of the first things I tell people when they ask for advice on starting a podcast is to talk about something you like talking about with someone you like talking about it with. In fact, the majority of my podcasts exist because I had a friend or family member that I wanted to make a show with and they were built from there. Justin already went over the "something you like talking about" part, so it's time to ask yourself: Do you want a cohost?

Don't get me wrong, there are definitely formats that are perfectly suited for one voice. For example, a biography podcast where you tell the stories of forgotten historical figures needs only one point of view and strong writing. However, if your podcast is discussion based in any way, you are doing yourself a huge disservice to try to carry on a one-person dialogue. Having another voice will:

A. Provide different points of view

B. Keep things moving

C. Make the audience feel like they are part of a conversation

I *always* have a cohost because I like having someone to talk to. It is great having someone there to pass the energy of the conversation back and forth. It keeps it from feeling like work.

Cohost Particulars

So, you've decided that you need a cohost! Next question: Is it a permanent cohost or a rotating guest? The big pro of the latter approach is you get a regular injection of new energy, perspective, and expertise. The big con? It will be harder for you (and the listener) to fall into a consistent groove. Each episode might be new and different, which may be viewed negatively by a listener who just wants to binge a bunch of eps back-to-back. That's not to say it *can't* work; it just depends on what the show calls for. If your intention is to make a show where each episode reflects the guest (like an interview show or a day-in-the-life show), then it's a perfect fit! Brace yourself, though; if your show is based on the guest, there will be listeners who skip episodes if they aren't interested in the person featured.

I have also known shows that have started with one host, done a bunch of episodes, and then realized that the show works better with two or more hosts. Don't be afraid to change things up if something isn't working.

One thing I will caution against is having too many voices on one show. If no one is able to get a word in, it's not going to be a very interesting discussion. I usually stick with two or three people, depending on the show. If the format is relaying information (like on *Shmanners*), I think two people are all you need. However, on *My Brother, My Brother and Me*, it really helps to have three so you have a chance to come up with jokes while the other two are talking.

One last piece of advice here: it's always easier to add a new person if the show needs it. Adding Courtney to *Trends Like These* was an absolute pleasure and brought an important new perspective to the show. It's a completely different beast to try to kick a friend off the show. I've been trying to kick Griffin off *My Brother, My Brother and Me* for years, and he still isn't getting the hint.

If you have decided to go it alone, good news! You get to skip ahead to discussing guests. If you have decided to work with one or more cohosts, even better news! You get to keep reading my beautiful prose. Before you get too far ahead of yourself, though, there are a few things you need to figure out.

First—and this might seem obvious—**are they interested in making a podcast with you?** Podcasting is a labor of love. It can require a lot of time researching, recording, editing, and publicizing. Are they ready to take that on? Podcasts can go on for hundreds of episodes (read: years). The last thing you want is to constantly have to bug your cohost to record and do the homework required for the show.

Next, **are they interested in the subject?** Just because they're your best friend and *you* find them super entertaining doesn't mean they are the right fit for your show. If they are your ideal cohost candidate, maybe work with them to develop a different show focused on a topic you both enjoy. There have been many shows that have found success with the "expert and novice" format, but even in that scenario it works best if all hosts involved find the topic interesting.

Are they available? If their schedule is too packed, it could make it nearly impossible to schedule a recording. It's not necessarily a deal breaker, but it's definitely a factor to be taken into consideration. That said, I know lots of shows that find a day where all the hosts are free and bulk-record a stockpile of episodes.

This one can be pretty hard to nail down, but **what is the nature of your chemistry?** If you find yourselves agreeing on everything, how will that impact the show? If you tend to argue, do you think that will benefit or impede the show?

Remember, a great friend does not inherently make a great cohost. Your chemistry may even be *too* good. Hear me out. While it can be fun to have a conversation with a friend where you finish each other's sentences, that isn't necessarily fun for the audience. Having fun recording with your best friend is great, but it's important to make sure you are including the audience in everything.

Include Different Points of View

When building a hosting team, I would encourage you to strive to include underrepresented voices, which can bring new information to the discussion and vastly improve the show. I had the idea to start *Trends Like These* with Brent because we had known each other for more than a decade, and we love discussing current events in an effort to understand them. However, we kept running into stories where we, as two cisgender men, had no frame of reference. I think the show didn't really click until we brought on Courtney. Not only is she an incredible host and commentator, but she also brought with her a wealth of life experience that Brent and I simply did not have. She was able to offer up insights that would have never crossed our minds. Including different voices in our creative endeavors is something we are still working to improve, so please learn from our mistakes!

Whether we're talking about cohosts or guests, it's important to clarify everyone's role. For some shows, one person assumes the role of the "expert" who explains the subject to the other host. Other shows involve a more balanced conversation among participants. Or maybe it's an interview show. Do the hosts play the role of news anchor, taking turns presenting stories to the listener? There are many different forms the conversation can take. Figuring out what roles everyone can fill will help the conversation flow smoothly.

Getting Together . . . Sort Of

A lot of podcasters don't put enough thought into the decision to record separately or in the same location. While being in the same room can often increase the chemistry with guests or among hosts, it can be easy to rely on body language and forget about the audience altogether, which may make the listener feel excluded. Recording in separate locations guarantees you are all reacting to the same stimulus as the listener and often means cleaner audio. If you are each on separate tracks in separate locations, you don't have to worry about one person's voice bleeding into another person's track. But my favorite part about remote recording is that it makes scheduling a whole lot easier! No one needs to worry about commuting to the studio, and it is easy to record on the spur of the moment if you find you suddenly have an hour of free time.

Obviously, there are downsides to recording in different locations. You can feel disconnected. Separate locations also means purchasing more equipment. More recording setups also means more opportunities for something to go wrong. This can be especially frustrating if one person involved, say the dad of the other cohosts, doesn't know how his computer works and keeps referring to it as "that box full of internet."

If one host lives in Orlando and the other lives in Seattle, you've really got only one option. If that is the case, don't worry! There are a couple of tips and tricks to help it go smoothly, but we'll get to those in a later chapter.

If you want to record in the same room, go for it! Just remember to keep your audience in mind. If it helps you remember to include them, you can even set up an empty chair as your surrogate audience member.

Guests, Who Needs Them? (Answer: Maybe You Do)

Let's talk about guests. Do you need them? There are many shows and formats that would be thrown off by adding an outside voice. Ask yourself: What would a guest add to the show? Would it work better if the guest joined for only a portion of the show instead of the whole episode?

One thing I would warn against is adding guests just to grow an audience. In my experience, it takes a *really* exciting guest to draw people in. Even then, it really only works if the guest does a lot of pushing when the episode comes out. It can work well if you have the guest scheduled and are able to publicize in advance to generate interest, but it's no guarantee. The problem is that talking about an exciting guest on your show only reaches people who are *already listening* to your show. You are counting on listeners to spread the word and bring in new folks, but that can be hit or miss. I suggest that rather than focusing on trying to get "big-name" guests, you should book guests who fit well with the attitude and chemistry of the show. The ideal being that a listener walks away thinking, "That was the best episode yet!" and tells all their friends about it.

When it comes to finding guests, start with people you know. If you have an entertaining friend or know an expert in a field, that's a great place to start! After that, the world is your oyster. Tweet or email performers you are a fan of to see if they are interested—it never hurts to ask. I suggest a short pitch, such as: "Hello, my name is [blank], and I host a podcast about [blank]. We were wondering if you might be interested in guesting sometime. Here's a link to an episode to give you an idea of what the show is all about: [link to your favorite episode]. Thanks so much!" Then, you wait. *Do not* tweet/email them nine times a day. That won't end well.

The Bones of a Show

WITH GRIFFIN MCELROY

So, you've got a concept! I'm sure it's gonna be a smash hit; another in a long line of runaway success stories of the lucrative podcasting industry. You've also got your hosts! Your chemistry is off the charts. This podcast house has great bones, you know? Now it's time to decide . . . how big . . . to make those bones. General bone-size stuff.

Up to this point, you've had to make some tough decisions about the fundamentals of your podcast. Now, it's time to actually structure your show and turn your idea into the real thing. It can be difficult to nail down without actually recording a dry run in earnest, feeling out what formula works best for the concept you've devised.

Nearly every podcast we've ever done has changed organically in the years we've been doing it. *My Brother, My Brother and Me* began as a forty-five-minute show where we would intro an episode, read questions from the audience and Yahoo Answers, and then outro the show. Over our first few months, the episode durations quickly grew to the hour-long format that we still adhere to today—a length of time that accommodated new segments, like an advertising block, and various recurring bits (like "Farm Wisdom" and Travis's much-despised "Sad Libs") that we began experimenting with in an attempt to add some variety to our standard formula.

Sometimes, it makes sense for your podcast not to have a hard-and-fast rule for how it's structured. *The Adventure Zone* is a good example of this; because it's a fiction podcast, each episode lasts as long as the story we're trying to tell. One of our episodes is thirty-seven minutes long. Our season one finale had a running time of two hours and forty-two minutes. Attempting to cap that show at a specific length would hinder the story we were trying to tell.

Scripted or Nonscripted?

Probably the biggest question you need to ask yourself when starting a podcast is: Scripted or nonscripted? You could find success with either, but try to choose the format that's a good fit for your skill set. There's a reason I've never made a scripted show: it seems really hard to write a bunch of words down ahead of time instead of making them up as I go along. I'm comfortable with my own limits.

I could always use a scripted podcast as an opportunity to

hone my abilities as a storyteller. But I'd need to get comfortable with the fact that there might not be a large audience of people who want to hear a grown man fumble through script writing until he found his feet.

In general, though, structure is good.

Podcast listening is a habitual behavior. You want the structure of your show to build expectations in your listeners' minds and reinforce their desire to participate in your show. If they listen to one episode and enjoy it, they'll expect to similarly enjoy your other episodes. If you can consistently deliver on that promise, you'll likely be able to turn your show's listeners into your show's subscribers.

Also, holy shit, having a structure makes recording dozens or hundreds of episodes of your podcast a much more palatable process.

The Adventure Zone is the most exhausting show that we create. Before we record, we have no idea what each episode is going to sound like when it's finished. If your show doesn't have consistent structure, you and your cohosts are going to be more likely to burn out, and the quality of your episodes is going to be all over the map. It's like you're building the plane beneath you every time you take it out to fly.

Just, like, generally speaking: this is bad for planes.

All of this is to say: figuring out a consistent structure for your show is as important as figuring out its concept and hosts—

but don't hesitate to tweak that structure during its early days until you find the composition that works best for you.

How Long Should My Podcast Be?

I dunno, probably an hour?

Next question.

Determining the perfect length for your podcast can be a real moving target when you're just starting out—and that's totally fine! Every podcast I've ever participated in has seen its running time fluctuate starting out, as my cohosts and I figured out what felt comfortable. Having a general idea of the scope of your show is a good idea, but don't sweat it if you don't settle on a target length right away. *Wonderful!*, the enthusiast show I do with my wife, Rachel, started as a half-hour podcast, but now it runs forty to fifty minutes, because that's just what feels *organic* and *good*.

In fact, adjusting this number early on is actually a pretty good practice. You may want to consider keeping your episodes on the shorter side when you're just starting out. In doing so, you increase your chances of new listeners actually finishing your earlier episodes, reinforcing the idea in their subconscious that if they finished listening to an episode of your show, they must have enjoyed it . . . right?

However, when trying to settle on a more permanent length for your podcast, there are two philosophical questions to ponder:

1. What's the ideal length of a show, based on average podcast consumption statistics?
2. What's the ideal length of my show, based on what feels right while recording it?

Trying to structure your show based solely on the first question will probably negatively impact your position on the second. Still, there's some interesting data out there relating to the average podcast listener's appetites that you should keep in mind when finding your show's formula.

Rob Walch, vice president of podcaster relations at Libsyn (one of the most popular podcast hosting platforms out there), shared some data at the 2017 National Association of Broadcasters convention in Las Vegas that seemingly supports the idea that longer shows can more effectively capture an audience's attention. According to Walch, 84 percent of podcasts that pull in more than one hundred thousand downloads per episode are longer than fifty-one minutes, while a little less than 10 percent are shorter than thirty minutes.

There's also some data about where people tune in to podcasts that appears to reinforce that assertion. In a 2017 survey conducted by polling firm Edison Research, 65 percent of folks who consume podcasts listen in their cars. If you factor in the average commute of an American worker—which, according to a recent U.S. Census Bureau poll, is about 25.5 minutes on average—there and back you arrive at that same fifty-one-minute mark touted by Walch.

As much as that sounds like a consensus, there are plenty of reasons not to use this data as a guideline for your show's length.

First off, it doesn't factor in the average length of all podcasts in existence. I don't know the average length of all podcasts ever, but anecdotally speaking, I listen almost exclusively to podcasts with running times over one hour. That has little to do with my preferences with regard to podcast length and more to do with the fact that there are simply more hour-long podcasts out there than half-hour-long podcasts. That discrepancy probably throws off the numbers a bit.

Also, while 65 percent of participants in Edison Research's poll listed their car as a listening destination, 84 percent said they also listened in their homes. There's also nothing saying the 65 percent who listen in their cars demand the podcast cover the entire duration of their drive time on a given day.

"Aaaah," Megan, an imaginary person I just made up, sighs as she pulls into her driveway, right as her favorite podcast wraps up another great episode. "Just how I, a completely fictional, nonexistent person, like it."

No, the far more important questions you need to ask yourself are: What's the correct length for my podcast? What best fits the topic? *The Memory Palace* works as a fifteen-minute-long show—it gets in, delivers a concise, powerful, intimate story, and gets out. *Hardcore History* works as a four- to five-hour-long show—it gets in, thoroughly covers the ever-living hell out of a subject, and gets out.

There's a good guideline to use that will help shape your show, regardless of its concept, and that's: How long will an episode of my show be entertaining to listen to? If you want to tell compelling short stories, your show should be short. If you want to tell exhaustive stories about every angle of a subject, it should be much longer. If you want to tell some jokes with your friends, it should be as long as you're able to deliver primo goofs in one sitting. Do not just fill for time—there's simply no need for it.

Throughout every step of creating your podcast, you'll be well served by harboring a deep respect for your audience's time. Let that, above anything else, determine the length of your show. Record a few episodes, allow yourself to be brutally honest about when it stops being entertaining, and wrap it up, right there.

Congratulations! You just discovered the length of your podcast.

What Kind of Segments Should My Podcast Have?

Rather than addressing the exact nature of the segments that would fit into your show—which would be impossible, because books are (unfortunately) a one-way method of transmitting information, and I do not know what kind of dark podcasting deeds you're plotting over there—I can share some general tips on how to create a consistent structure that your listeners will learn to rely on.

The Beginning and the End

Each episode should have an intro and an outro, natch. Both should ideally have some kind of musical accompaniment—a genuine banger that matches and establishes the aesthetic of the show you perform (we'll have more on that much later). Your intro should do what it says on the tin: introduce the title of the show and its hosts, and establish the tone or topic of the podcast episode your listeners are about to hear.

A general comedy show might start things off with a cold open, just making off-the-cuff goofs about whatever before transitioning to the rest of the episode. A more personality-driven show might begin with an update on the hosts' lives before diving in. An educational show might open with a prewritten stage setter for the topic of conversation. Regardless of what you choose, your intro should be entertaining, succinct, and, at the bare minimum, explain who you are and what you do.

Don't take that last bit for granted: you never know which episode will be the first one someone decides to tune in to.

You should keep your outro just as uniform as your intro

between episodes. General consensus is that this is the ideal time to include plugs for your other projects, various social media handles, or whatever, as well as a call to action for listeners to leave reviews and share the show with their friends. However, don't belabor this section: you don't want to make it insurmountable, which will guarantee that your listeners will tune out early.

The Middle

The body of your podcast episode will be where the sausage gets made. The sausage of your . . . idea meat. It can be extremely helpful to compartmentalize this section when possible. The majority of an episode of *My Brother, My Brother and Me* is made up of listener questions and Yahoo Answers—when one of those starts to drag, we're able to quickly pivot to the other, repeating this cycle until we approach the average running time of our show. This setup gives us a lot of control over the general direction of each episode while we're still in the middle of creating it.

It's worth mentioning that your transitions between segments don't always have to be codified mile markers for the listener. On *My Brother, My Brother and Me*, we're usually pretty explicit about when a new question or segment is about to begin. On *Sawbones*, Justin and Sydnee don't really make a big deal out of signposting their transitions; they simply keep the next segment in mind, ready to hop over whenever the conversation starts to drag.

Again, audiences enjoy podcasts that fulfill their expectations, as established by the other episodes of that podcast they've listened to. Random one-off segments deployed hither and yon across your show can be jarring to your audience and cause friction in their listening experience. Keep in mind that your show is free. There's nothing keeping a listener from unsubscribing, making it all the more vital that you avoid introducing any kind of listener friction like the plague.

That's not to say you shouldn't occasionally try to mix things up to keep your show fresh! But you should probably do it only if that new segment painlessly fits into the show you're already making and if you plan to incorporate it on some kind of recurring basis.

And on a related note, if a bit isn't working, don't hesitate to drop it and start experimenting with something new. In addition, if your segments are reliant on things like news stories or other timely topics, and you're unable to find anything good for a given episode, you should probably just skip said segment for that week rather than simply phoning it in.

Advertising Breaks

Regarding advertising blocks: almost nobody likes them. You probably won't have to worry about this if you're just starting out or simply planning on podcasting as a hobby. If they do become a part of your show, though, keep them concise, entertaining, and clearly separated—perhaps with a quick bit of music—from the rest of the episode's content.

Troubleshooting Your Format

Having multiple segments can help you troubleshoot any weaknesses you identify in the content of your show. Finding it difficult to keep your discussions on a movie recap podcast entertaining start to finish? Add some segments to break up the conversation! Having a hard time engaging your podcast's growing fanbase? Introduce a segment that gives them some kind of voice on the show! *Jordan, Jesse, Go!* accomplishes this with a "Momentous Occasions" segment, where fans call in to talk about a great, funny thing they saw recently. It's hysterical and also a really good way to get listeners invested.

How Often Should I Release Episodes?

When figuring out a release schedule, you should keep two factors in mind.

First, the logistical considerations: How often can I get my hosts together to record? How long do we need to prep each episode? How long does postproduction take on each episode?

How rich of a vein is the subject of my podcast? Will we run the risk of burning through all our potential topics if we release too frequently?

You probably won't be able to make the exact calculation on those questions before you've recorded your first episode, but you should at least know enough to decide between the small handful of logical options: weekly, biweekly, or monthly.

The longer you go without releasing an episode, the more likely it is that you'll interrupt your subscribers' listening habits—you should really go that route only if you're producing a show with appointment listening. Is your show super high-touch, beefy, and not reliant on remembering things from past episodes in order to dive back in? A longer gap between releases probably makes more sense. Is it competing in the already packed comedy podcast market, and, production-wise, is it a fairly light lift? You'll probably want to target a pretty tight turnaround.

That said, the more important thing to keep in mind is the second factor, which is: How frequently can I consistently release new episodes?

One of the best ways to maintain subscriber retention is to allow your listeners to build your show into their regular routines. Maybe you're their constant companion during their Monday morning commute. Maybe you're how they kick off their weekends on Friday afternoons. Maybe they listen to your recap podcast first thing in the morning after whatever it is you're recapping. Regardless, interrupting this pattern by skipping episodes or publishing off schedule is a surefire way to lose listeners, either in the short term or, if you consistently miss your established deadlines, permanently.

On weeks where we publish *My Brother, My Brother and Me* late—which is to say, not on Monday mornings—our download count for that episode invariably takes a hit. When we miss an episode entirely (which we try like the dickens to never do), it takes a few weeks for our download count to recover, for folks to get back into the "routine" of listening to our show.

If a weekly recording and editing schedule seems too rigorous to maintain, then by all means, do not attempt it. A biweekly or monthly publishing schedule can just as easily establish a routine with the listener. For *The Adventure Zone*, we realized very early on how difficult it would be to produce that show every week. Despite the fact that we moved to a biweekly schedule, the download count for that show hasn't suffered—it just built a different expectation in our audience.

Whichever kind of schedule you establish for your show, there's one target you should try to hit: publish new episodes of your podcast in the morning. If you're on Pacific time, you might want to consider uploading the file and setting it to publish automatically for the morning of Eastern time. Not everyone listens to podcasts during their morning commute, but it's generally a good idea to have your show ready for those who do.

I realize there's a lot to unpack in this section and that a lot of it seems like pure guesswork, given that you haven't actually sat down to record a proper episode yet. My recommendation is to do just that: record a trial episode that you don't plan on releasing. Get a feel for your and your cohosts' dynamics and figure out what kind of segments are fun to play around with. Have an honest conversation about how often you can rely on one another to consistently get together and record.

And then, at the end of that trial, if the episode you recorded isn't as spectacular as you were hoping, throw it in the garbage! Nobody has to know.

Research

**WITH SYDNEE MCELROY,
TERESA MCELROY, AND RACHEL MCELROY**

 Interested in creating a podcast that has a research component? Don't look to us for guidance. Research is hard, so we don't do it. Luckily, we have far more capable and intelligent wives who have taken that up. I asked my wife, Dr. Sydnee McElroy, to handle this chapter, with help from Travis's *Shmanners* cohost and wife, Teresa McElroy, and Griffin's *Wonderful!* cohost and wife, Rachel McElroy.

SYDNEE
MCELROY

Initially, when Justin asked me to help write this section on research, I was reluctant. I do not consider myself a professional researcher, and, as I state often on our show *Sawbones: A Marital Tour of Misguided Medicine*, I am *far* from a historian. But here I am, seven years later, the host of a medical history podcast, still releasing new episodes every week. So perhaps I am uniquely qualified to discuss this very specific type of podcast research.

What Is Your Goal?

If research seems like an intimidating prospect, that's because it is! That's why it's really important that you decide on the mission of your show before you start. I knew from the beginning that I could not provide an in-depth, comprehensive history of, say, cholera or vasectomies in a thirty-minute podcast. Nor was I particularly interested in doing that, as it would have relegated Justin to the sidelines. You don't find a lot of humorous sidebars in academic journals or textbooks (though I would make the case that this is unfortunate).

A very simple way of making this choice is by deciding on a genre. We set out to make a comedy podcast. While I intended to include plenty of interesting facts that would inform the listener, the primary mission was to entertain. After listening to an episode of *Sawbones*, the listener has hopefully had some laughs and, perhaps, feels better equipped for pub trivia. But they're not necessarily an expert on the week's subject matter.

TERESA
MCELROY

When we made a pilot show for *Shmanners*, I kept couching everything with "I'm not an expert," thinking that because I wasn't formally published in or didn't hold any degrees in etiquette (does that even exist?) I wasn't qualified to make a podcast. But, after sending it out to people for critique, the overwhelming response was that I *was* an expert—after I did my research, that is. That's not to say that I don't make mistakes, but I enter into a contract with the listener that I've done the work to ensure I know what I'm talking about.

If you do want to make a show where the primary purpose is to educate your audience on a specific subject in a comprehensive manner, you may need help. There are many podcasters who work with whole teams of researchers to fact-check their show and provide them with relevant sources. From the beginning, I knew I would not have the time or the resources for this approach. When we first started *Sawbones*, I was working full-time as a practicing family physician. We also had our oldest child during the first year of our show. Suffice it to say, researching and recording our podcast was far from the only thing on my plate. Learning about medical history was and still is a hobby for me, and *Sawbones* provides me with a very structured opportunity to indulge this very peculiar curiosity.

We started *Shmanners* while I was pregnant with our first child. I was doing all the prep for it until I became pregnant with our second. Now, our show uses a research assistant. Together, we'll discuss the focus of the show, and then she will gather the information. Sometimes, I'll send her articles I find interesting, and then she'll write the script. Having another researcher in the mix helps make these shows more enjoyable for our audience (and for myself!).

In lieu of a whole team, I would advise keeping your topics narrow and your episodes short. You could also create a show that covers more ground and releases less frequently. While my goal is not to make a purely educational medical podcast, I am familiar with many podcasts that release extremely short episodes, providing bite-size, concentrated, up-to-date important information on a particular topic.

If you do want to tackle something a little more akin to "infotainment," you can easily go it alone. In approaching the research, your focus should be on accuracy as opposed to breadth. If I am covering the history of bloodletting, I don't need to locate every historical reference of its use and provide a complete chronological account, but I do need to ensure that the instances that I choose to highlight are factual. When you are doing a research-based show, there is an implicit understanding that the information you are providing is true, to the best of your abilities. It is important to honor that agreement. Or you will get emails. *Lots* of emails.

RACHEL MCELROY

I think it's also fair to mention that, when selecting your goal, you should consider what you as a host can uniquely bring toward meeting that goal. If you're starting with limited expertise, you're setting yourself up for a lot more research. When I started *Wonderful!* with Griffin, we were riding the coattails of a previous show, *Rose Buddies*, that focused on recapping and critiquing reality dating shows. We started with that show partially because I felt, with the support of Griffin, that we were uniquely qualified to comment on these programs given our vast knowledge of *The Bachelor*. The only research that was required was watching the episode and taking notes. Our goal was to entertain, but as the reality dating shows became less entertaining and more concerning (trust me), we pivoted to *Wonderful!*, a podcast about, well, all the things we think are wonderful. While the goal is still to entertain, the breadth of focus gives us far more control over what we can discuss. It also allows us to choose topics that we already know a fair amount about. The research then becomes something to supplement existing knowledge, making it more interesting to both us and listeners. Because when we're genuinely interested and excited, it's more likely that the audience will be too.

Finding Individual Topics

Choosing episode topics is generally pretty easy in the beginning. You started the show because of your interest in a subject, so you probably already had a bunch of ideas for episodes before you even started recording the show. Over time, when that well of initial ideas starts to dry up, it has the potential to become more difficult, which is why I suggest enlisting the help of your audience. I don't remember if we had explicitly asked listeners to email the show with their own topic ideas or if it just happened naturally, but I am eternally grateful for it. The majority of our show topics come from listener suggestions now, so choosing one is never a concern.

For *Shmanners*, we have always relied heavily on listener suggestions. The focus of our show is on societal behavior, so while the topics we choose are often rooted in history, they are relevant to our listeners today.

It is important that you do some light research on a potential topic before you nail it down. I have wasted many research hours trying to make a show out of something that just isn't going to work. Sometimes, it turns out the topic is too narrow and there won't be enough content to fill the episode. Occasionally, it will turn out that an area of history that seemed very exciting is actually pretty mundane or even a total bummer. Since Justin's job is to make jokes about the information I'm presenting, topics that are total bummers don't make his job very easy. Whatever the reason, if you start to dig into an idea and find there's nothing there, be prepared to abandon it and pivot to something else. Not everything makes a good podcast episode.

This is where it's helpful to return to your goal. If your goal is to entertain listeners, for example, it's important to choose topics that will primarily be entertaining. Is your topic so complicated that you're going to spend most of your time lecturing? Is your topic so simple that you've got very little to say about it? Is there another podcast already talking about this topic from a more informed and experienced perspective? If any of these are true, it's less likely your show is going to stand out. Often, I'll be drawn to topics that I think are fascinating, but after some research I'll realize I don't have anything unique to say about it. Or sometimes I'll realize, after a thorough investigation, that the thing I wanted to discuss is more fraught than I initially expected. If this is the case, it will come through in your show.

Finding Your Information

Once you've done some initial reading and feel like there's enough stuff out there to support a whole episode, find a good summary article. There is no shame in using Wikipedia as a starting point, but there is shame in also using it as your ending point. The other advantage to starting with a summary article is that it will generally include a list of references. This is where you can really start branching out into new information for your listeners. Follow the links to other articles, books, journals, primary sources, etc. *Then* you can begin to form a more complete outline in your mind before trying to translate it to an audience.

Because my show is about medical history, I look to medical and scientific journals for a lot of my information. This is nice for a couple of reasons. First, they are generally peer-reviewed and referenced, so I feel confident about the accuracy of the information being presented. Second, the bibliographies provide lots of great opportunities for digging further into the topic. The disadvantage here is that many journal articles are available only with a subscription or if you pay for the individual article itself. For my purposes, it has been cost-effective to subscribe to several journals that I find myself returning to frequently.

The internet is full of etiquette blogs, but I find myself sticking to more tried-and-true sources like the Emily Post Institute, Miss Manners columns, and *Smithsonian* magazine articles. I have also amassed a large library of books, but I rely on those for procedural advice and historical perspective. Our show is more about the "how to feel good doing it" and less about the "do it this way or else."

One benefit of choosing to do a podcast about something you are already genuinely interested in is that your hobby can fuel your show. I have a fairly large library of medical history books that I have happily invested in throughout the years we have been making our show. Having access to my own reference library has cut down on the time I need to spend digging around for information, but I also just enjoy reading them.

After you accumulate your sources, I would advise reading them thoroughly before you start outlining the show itself. I do not type (or record) a single word until I have read at least a handful of articles or book chapters on the topic. You cannot communicate anything to your audience until you understand the complete story.

When I'm at the point where I feel like I know what I want to say, I'll start generating a two- to three-page document summarizing the key dates, figures, and/or events that I want to focus on to keep myself on track. While I do not write what I want to say verbatim, I do give myself clues and key words in the outline as to what idea I am trying to convey by presenting that particular piece of information. I have never done a scripted podcast, but I am certain this step would take far longer were I to make that sort of show.

I do rely on the script written by our brilliant research assistant, but I hardly ever read it word for word. When I first started out, I did a lot of copying and pasting from other sources, but it was hard to create the fully fleshed-out story that Sydnee describes, and that is so important. Personally,

I enjoy the voice and tone of our researcher's scripts, so I am genuinely happy to present them. Or present them as much as I can—Travis provides a lot of derailing commentary because that's his role on our show.

When I research, I always err on the side of too much material, so that I can pare down the content prior to making the show. The process of paring down helps me become more familiar with the topic and also better understand what information is essential to telling the story. Oftentimes, I'll find myself debating whether a particular event or milestone is necessary to the topic, which usually means we'll be fine without it. I will also think about whether the information is likely to elicit any response from my cohost, Griffin. This is why it's a huge asset to know your cohost really well. If you have a fact that you think might be interesting but is unlikely to inspire your cohost, you will probably want to just leave it out. Your audience will ultimately appreciate it.

Finding Your Story

It took me a few months of actually creating the show before I began to realize what made an episode particularly enjoyable. Our early shows were largely deep dives into particularly wacky medical treatments or discussions of a shifting diagnosis throughout history. There was not necessarily an overarching story, and the focus of my research was very much on finding the grossest or weirdest things humans have done in the past and presenting them to the audience. After a few biographical episodes received some especially positive attention from listeners, I started to see what made those shows better. A person's life naturally has a story, which means there is a built-in narrative arc.

I knew I didn't want to focus the entire podcast on historical figures, so instead I started trying to find the story within each topic I researched. Whatever the subject matter—whether it be a person, a disease, a type of medicine, or a fixed time period—there is a hook somewhere in there that listeners will recognize as plot and connect to instantly. If I have one piece of wisdom about conducting research for podcasts, it is this: find the story. Until you find the story, your research will just be a collection of facts. They may be very true and very interesting to you and provide excellent fodder with which your funny cohost can make jokes, but those episodes will not speak to your audience in the same way that a good story can.

In order to achieve this, I believe you have to do two things well. First, you have to read about the subject with an open mind, without trying to synthesize or structure the data. Just read and learn and let all the information fill your brain until you feel really comfortable with the basic gist of things. It's like a puzzle—the big picture will become clear to you only once you have a really good sense of the pieces.

This leads me to the second thing you have to do well, which I personally feel is the hardest part: be willing to scrap a lot of what you've learned for the sake of the show. Just tell the story and leave all that other research for your own edification. Or make another episode out of it some other time, I suppose.

> Travis usually does this for me while we record the show. He will find a few things to discuss off the cuff and turn it into the best part. He is the comedian and I am the straight man of our duo. I can't even count the number of times I have abandoned whole sections of facts because he jumped to the good part—and I usually have to follow him.

This can be really hard to do, so let me elaborate a little. For example, I will realize that while a treatment may have its roots in ancient Greece, the most interesting thing about it happened in the sixteenth century. In which case, I have learned to let go of all the other facts and articles I have accumulated in service to the *real story*. I may make a brief mention of the treatment's Greek origins or etymology, or throw in a nod to Pliny the Elder (because I know how much our consistent listeners love that guy), but I will focus the whole show on just that sixteenth-century story. These episodes are almost always our best. This also speaks to my initial point about deciding what the purpose of your podcast is. If I set out to tell the comprehensive history of a given topic, I would not have this freedom. However, by allowing the information to dictate the content of the show, I can limit the show to the best stories and leave the listeners to investigate more if they so choose.

I often get bogged down in history because that's the part I like the best. It doesn't always serve our purposes because, with *Shmanners*, what our listeners want is actionable instruction, and frankly, that's the reason they listen. Our best shows have the two halves of "here's what history says about it" and "here's how you can use this information."

On *Wonderful!*, I have a segment called "Rachel's Poetry Corner" that's focused on a particular poet and poem that I enjoy. When I started this segment, I had many poems ready in hand from my favorite poets. These were poems and poets that I had studied in college and graduate school, so the research and story came easily to me. As the segment continued, I found myself having to draw deeper down into my reservoir of poets and begin featuring poems that I knew less about. Often there was only one poem or one fact that I had on reserve prior to researching. This made my story less clear and the task of putting together a cohesive narrative around a poem or poet more daunting. Now I've developed a framework of questions that help me get to the story quicker. Where is this person I'm talking about from, and how did that influence who they ultimately became? What are the major achievements of this person that make them impressive to me? What artists, writers, etc., influenced them? What makes their work uniquely appealing to me? If the answers to these questions are accessible and relatable, the outline of my story will be nearly complete.

My Mistakes

This brings to mind a few mistakes I have made along the way that, perhaps, you can avoid.

When it comes to ensuring accuracy, cross-referencing is your best tool. Basic dates and names probably don't need more than a couple references, but if it is a fact that seems especially sensational or strange, look for documentation of it in several other sources. In addition, look to see where *those* sources got the information as well. On one occasion, I found a fact about ancient attitudes toward C-sections repeated in multiple different sources, only to be called out by listeners who let me know it was actually a myth. I went back to my sources and found that they were all quoting the same mistaken article. Again, not every single piece of information needs this much checking, but if something sounds like it can't possibly be true, do the work to prove it to yourself before sharing it with others.

One thing I still don't do consistently, but wish I had done from the very beginning, is keep a list of my resources for each episode. That can come in handy if, say, you are asked to write a book based on your episodes someday. Then you will really wish you had done this. It could also help with future episodes. Whether you choose to share that list with your audience for their personal enjoyment is up to you. I will say, for what it's worth, that I am frequently asked to share my sources, and I don't have any solid philosophical reason not to do so. I hated compiling bibliographies as a student and had sworn never to do it again unless forced by a teacher . . . but here we are.

Finally, as much as I hate to admit it, I have gotten things wrong before. As diligent as I try to be, the amount of information we have accessible electronically these days makes it hard not to include a much-repeated myth-as-fact every so often. When this has happened, I have confirmed my mistake and owned up to it immediately. Often, I will start our next episode off with a correction, so that the misinformation does not persist. I have found that by acknowledging when I get something wrong, my listeners will continue to trust me to get most things right.

My biggest mistake is putting the delivery of the research before my primary responsibility of being a charming host and partner to my cohost. It is not unusual for me to find myself in the middle of a dense factoid when I have to remind myself, "People aren't coming here to listen to a book report, they're coming to hear you talk to Griffin." Nobody is going to miss the research you didn't get to share. Your listeners aren't going to be like, "The person the host mentioned died in 1972, but the host stopped discussing her achievements when she reached 1961!" Don't forget to put down the notes and play with your partner in the space. That's probably why you started making this show, right?

That's All There Is to It

If all of this sounds overwhelming, please keep in mind that while I was trained in basic research methods in medical school and I have had some practice with lecturing through my job as an assistant professor, most of what I have learned has been through *trial and error.* You *don't* have to be an expert on something to do a podcast about it. You *do* have to be enthusiastic about it, though.

My training is from the opposite end of the spectrum. I have an acting degree, so I've always felt comfortable with public speaking. I play the role of a teacher on *Shmanners*, so I had to become one. This is hardly the first time I've done this; my first career was as a swim teacher and lifeguard instructor. Not to belabor Sydnee's point, but I too have a pupil in my cohost that makes it easy and fun to teach, but once again, that's another section.

While I'm not a teacher by trade, I come from a long line of professional educators, and I currently work in higher education administration. I know that the best teachers are the people who hold on to their curiosity and their vulnerability. A podcast is an opportunity to intimately teach a listener about our world and ourselves, and this is most effective when we bring our feelings to the table. Ultimately, the research you do as a host is research your listeners could do on their own if they were so motivated. This can be embarrassing to admit and may make you want to throw in the towel. But the strength behind your research is in how you present it—you are uniquely you with your voice and your spirit. With this in mind, you just have to figure out how you're going to share yourself with the listeners so that they not only want to learn about the topic, but they specifically want to learn about the topic from *you*.

So, what do I do? I find the things that interest me and try to lay out the facts of the stories in interesting ways. I attempt to do justice to the people and events that I share with my listeners and connect the past to the present with universal themes and empathy. I also have the advantage of a cohost whom I feel very comfortable sharing my quirky interests with and whom I trust to see the humor in what I'm presenting, but that goes beyond the bounds of this book section to which I was assigned.

Though I encouraged Sydnee to please feel free to take up more of the book singing my praises, she refused. I have requested that the publisher leave the next thirty pages blank so that the reader can imagine her thorough, touching account of my talents.

CHAPTER TWO
Tools

Hardware

WITH TRAVIS MCELROY

We're going to dive deep into the world of hardware here. If that sounds boring to you, you are very wrong! Once you learn a few basics, you'll fall in love with this stuff just like I did.

If you are going to start a podcast, you are going to need a device to record it. You could try just going to every listener's home to perform the podcast live, but I wouldn't recommend it. The world of microphones and other audio devices can be daunting because of the wide array of options, so we're going to do our best to simplify things by category.

Microphones

First, let's start with the big one: **MICROPHONES!** When we started *My Brother, My Brother and Me,* Griffin was using the microphone that came with the video game *Rock Band,* and I was using a $15 combo headset/microphone that I got at Walmart. We would have gotten better audio quality if we had recorded using paper cups tied to pieces of twine. If you want an example of what you *don't* want your audio to sound like, just listen to the first twenty episodes of *My Brother, My Brother and Me.* Just kidding! No one should ever listen to the first twenty episodes of *My Brother, My Brother and Me.* You know what, just skip to the mid-200s.

Since those horrible, horrible days, we have been on a search for the best microphone option for podcasting. In order to understand our recommendations, there's some technical stuff we need to run you through. Try not to fall asleep.

There are three main types of microphones. I'm going to give you a pretty simplified description of each because I am no expert, and I'm guessing you aren't either! They are as follows:

- **Dynamic Mics:** The workhorse of the mic world, dynamics tend to be sturdy and reliable. If you walk into any theater or live show venue, ninety-nine times out of a hundred you are going to find a dynamic mic in use. They do not require power to operate (more on that in a second) and can work in a studio setting or onstage. They aren't as specialized as a condenser microphone, but they get the job done.

- **Condenser Mics:** Condenser mics pick up more detail than dynamics, but as such can require more fine-tuning in your gain settings. Condenser mics also require 48 volts of power to operate; this is referred to as "phantom power." That means you can't just plug a condenser mic into a computer and start using it. You are going to need a soundboard or some kind of interface between the mic and your recording device to provide those 48 volts. Condenser mics do very well in studio settings, especially for voice-over work and podcasting.

- **Ribbon Mics:** Ribbon mics are decidedly old school. They fell out of favor for a while, but there has been renewed interest in them recently. They are less sensitive to higher frequencies and tend to capture them without a lot of harshness. They're great if you are going for a vintage-y feel in your recordings.

Recording Patterns

Recording patterns (sometimes called "polar patterns") are the shape of the area that the microphone picks up sound from. Dynamic, condenser, and ribbon mics can come in any pattern you need.

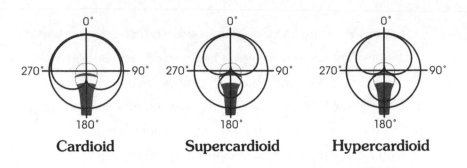

| Cardioid | Supercardioid | Hypercardioid |

- **Cardioid:** Imagine blowing a bubble and you'll be picturing a cardioid pattern. This means that the microphone is mainly picking up the sound directly in front of it. It will pick up some surrounding noise (that is how sound works, microphones are not magic), but it's mostly only going to pick up sound from the person talking directly into it. This is perfect for scenarios where each person has their own microphone. There are also cardioid variations called supercardioid and hypercardioid. The super pattern has a slightly narrower field in front and a small bulb of sensitivity in the back. Hyper has an even narrower front field and a larger back field, which creates a more precise sound pickup but requires careful mic technique. In other words, when using this mic, if the sound being recorded moves off-center a little, you might lose it.

- **Omnidirectional:** Well, it says it right there in the name! This pattern is a circle of sensitivity with the microphone in

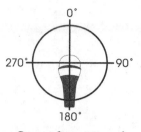

Omnidirectional

the middle. It picks up sound in every direction at equal levels. This is ideal in a scenario where you use only one microphone to record a bunch of people at the same time. It is trickier to get a "clean" recording with omnidirectional, though, so if you plan on using this mic, it's even more important that you choose a place to record without a bunch of ambient noise.

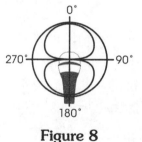

Figure 8

- **Figure 8:** With a figure 8, there is an area of sensitivity at the front of the mic and the back of the mic with very limited areas on the sides. This is great for a scenario in which there are only two people being recorded at the same time, though it's not the best solution for a two-person recording, as it requires them to crowd around one mic. But it works great in a pinch.

Are you still with me? We're almost done with the technical stuff, I swear! Only one last thing.

Cable Connections

How does your microphone connect to your recording device? Just like before, you can find all kinds of different mics with varying sound patterns that use either USB or XLR.

- **USB:** Simple to set up, a USB microphone cable plugs directly into your computer. Settings can be adjusted either on the microphone itself or through your computer. You have a lot less control over the recording, but it is also incredibly easy to get rolling. Though it's the more straightforward option, only one USB mic can be connected at a time. If you want more, you'll need . . .
- **XLR:** This is probably what most people would think of as a microphone cable. This cable connects to the mic and then into an amplifier, soundboard, or any kind of audio interface. Your recording will either be stored on a memory card in your interface or be saved to a connected computer. Because that interface serves as a middleman, you are usually able to tweak the recording way more than you would be able to with a USB connection. It can be the difference between one knob on the microphone versus thirty knobs on a soundboard. If you want to use more than one microphone in your recording, XLR is the only way (unless you want to involve multiple computers).

See, that wasn't so bad! Now we can get into the fun stuff . . . *shopping*! You probably want to know which mic is best to start with. Well, it's not really that cut and dry. First, you have to ask yourself: How committed are you to podcasting? If you want to try recording an episode or two or ten before you overcommit yourself, I would recommend a USB microphone in the lower-end range ($100 or less). There is a brand called Blue that has some really great, reasonably priced options. It might be a little awkward for you and your cohosts to keep taking turns talking into one mic, and the sound won't be top-level studio quality, but you'll be able to explore your newfound hobby without breaking the bank.

Here's what I would *not* recommend as a budget option: a set of XLR mics for less than $40. It doesn't sound like a lot at first, until you add in all the money you're going to have to spend on cables and an audio interface (more on this in a moment). Getting a set of XLR mics should feel like an investment. When I first started podcasting, I made the mistake of always buying the cheapest set and then replacing it every time I could afford better. If I had just invested in a good-quality set of XLR mics to begin with, I would have saved a whole lot of money.

If you are ready to invest a little bit more in a USB mic, I highly recommend the Blue Yeti, which goes for about $130. Not only is the quality relatively good for the price, but you can also adjust the recording patterns among stereo (this is also called binaural; ASMR creators use this a lot), omnidirectional, cardioid, and figure 8. It's a really versatile mic and very easy to set up.

It can be easy to get the impression that USB mics = low quality and XLR mics = good quality. This is not always the case. I used a USB mic for many years and was perfectly happy with it. I made the switch to XLR because I started recording with cohosts in the same room and I found that was easier to do with multiple microphones. To reiterate, you can really only use one USB mic at a time.

So, let's say you are looking to switch from USB to XLR or you have decided to start with XLRs. There are some additional things you are going to need. First, you are going to need cables, XLR male-to-female cables specifically (the terminology is gross, I know). A good six-foot-long XLR cable is pretty affordable. Cables can be deceptively important when it comes to audio quality. I have found that a lot of audio issues end up being caused by loose connections or shorts in cables. I would also recommend having a few spare cables around; they can wear out over time (especially if you find yourself unplugging/replugging a lot). You would be amazed at how many times the answer to a technical or audio issue is "replace the cable."

So now it's finally time to discuss **audio interfaces**. Simply put, you plug your microphone into an audio interface and you plug the audio interface into your computer. They can range from a simple box with one input and one knob to a behemoth with a bajillion inputs, knobs, and switches. A simple interface isn't going to break the bank, and a good-quality soundboard is going to start at around $100.

If you are like me, you may be looking to throw your whole self into podcasting right away and buy the "best" (read: most expensive) stuff right away. I would strongly warn against it. First, if you are inexperienced with a soundboard, one knob on the box interface is going to do you just as much good. Second, there's no reason to splurge on a ton of expensive equipment before you know that you want to continue.

That said . . .

When you are ready to make that kind of investment, I highly recommend that you consider purchasing a Zoom. The Zoom, available in models H1 to H6, is a sound interface, recording device, and microphone all in one handheld machine. It's perfect when recording audio at home or on the go. I have an H6, and I love it more than I love most people.

I hear you right now screaming, "*Travis!* Enough of this malarkey! Just tell me which mic to buy!" First off, there's no need for that kind of language. Second, okay, you win! Here's my suggestion . . .

The Shure SM58. I would say that nine out of every ten theaters we've done live shows at use them. Not only does the SM58 have good sound quality, it's also very sturdy. Unless you are actively trying to destroy it, it's going to last you a good long time. Now, the SM58 is going to cost you about $100, but it is totally worth it. So, if you are looking to get a set of mics for you and your cohosts and are willing to make an investment, this is the way I would go.

You may be wondering, "What kind of mics do the McElroys use?" We use CAD E100S microphones. We have tried out *so* many different mics, and we find that these work best with our voices and how we want our podcasts to sound. If you are really looking to make an investment and you want to sound like our show, there you go.

Now, let me tell you the dirty little microphone secret: more expensive doesn't inherently mean better. Sure, you're going to notice the difference between a $10 mic and a $500 mic. But what about between a $400 mic and a $500 mic? My rule of thumb is that once you get above $100, it comes down to personal preference. You might prefer the sound quality of a $200 mic over the $400 mic, and that's totally valid. How do you know before you buy? Good news! There is a metric ton of microphone demos on YouTube that you can check out. Just search for the model you are looking for and have fun!

One last thing! An often-overlooked mic option is a lavalier or lapel mic. I have had success with a wired model that plugs directly into the XLR ports. I find this to be a perfect option if you are doing an interview-style podcast. You can easily clip the mic on to the guest and move on, which saves them from having to hold on to a mic or stay still in front of a stand. There tends to be a bit of a decrease in quality (these pick up a lot of background noise in my experience) but might be worth it for ease of use!

So, you've got your cables, interface, and microphones. Now, what else do you need?

Microphone Stands

You've got a couple options here. First, ask yourself: Do you want desktop stands or floor stands? The pros of a desktop stand are that it is compact, and if you are sitting at a table, it's easy to position right in front of you. The con is that it will pick up vibrations and noise when you hit the table. The pros of a floor stand are you don't have to worry every time you put your hands down on the table and it's the only option if you are going to be standing up to record. The cons are that it's larger and more cumbersome to position.

You can also decide between an articulated/scissor arm and a fixed stand. The scissor arm gives you a lot more maneuverability, but it is also a lot more sensitive to vibration sound. The fixed stand is sturdier but is limited in its positioning.

Headphones

I love headphones! There, I said it. It feels so good to finally get that off my chest. There are lots of people out there who don't appreciate headphones as podcasting essentials, but not the McElroys. We use headphones in every single recording. This is partly because we are all in different locations and calling each other. However, even if we were recording in the same room, we would still consider headphones a pivotal part of podcasting production. Wearing headphones to hear your cohosts can improve the show in myriad ways. First, it can help you dial in and pay better attention to the conversation. It also allows you to hear the conversation the way the audience will be hearing it. You can monitor levels to make sure no one is too loud or too quiet. It can also help find audio issues that you may not be able to detect just by looking at the audio track.

No matter what, you should be editing the show using headphones. Once again, that is how most people are going to listen to the finished product, so it's how you should be analyzing it. Whether recording or editing, I strongly recommend over-ear headphones. They reduce sound bleed when recording and allow for more isolation of sound when editing. Sound bleed is when you can hear the sound coming through the headphones in the recording. It creates a weird echo and can ruin a recording. If you are looking for more ways to avoid sound bleed, be sure to turn your headphone levels as low as you can.

If you are going to use headphones for recording with multiple people in the same room, be sure to get yourself a headphone splitter. A splitter is a cable that you can plug multiple headphones into and then plug that cable into one source. They range from a two-way splitter to a five-way splitter to a powered four-way splitter that allows you to set individual levels for each pair of headphones.

Windscreens and Soundproofing

At a bare minimum, you should get some foam covers for your microphones. I recommend getting the multicolored ones for reasons that I will explain in the next section. You might also opt to get yourself a windscreen. A windscreen is a thin layer of fabric stretched over a ring that you put between your mouth and the mic. If you, like me, have powerful plosives ($p/k/t/g/b/d$ sounds), then this becomes a must-have.

There are also soundproofing options (foam squares, curtains, a panel that attaches to the mic stand) to help with your recording space, but I have found these to be, for the most part, unnecessary. They are effective, but podcasting doesn't usually require a super pro sound quality level. However, if you are attempting to set up a full-blown recording studio space, it's worth looking into.

Other Random Equipment

Get yourself a set of multicolored electrical tape and thank me later. You are going to use it to color-code your cables with your mic foam covers so you can quickly adjust levels for each mic without having to track which cables go where. You're welcome.

You are also going to want to get a dog training clicker. While that sounds weird, it can make editing way easier. While recording, if you have an edit point, just add a few clicks right into the mic! When you are editing later, it will be very easy to spot the clicks in your track. Along those same lines, keep a notepad and pen nearby so you can make note of time codes for edits.

Looking for a pro-caster maneuver? Get yourself a cough button, my friend. Just like it sounds, it's a button you can push to mute your mic while you cough, sneeze, take a phone call, or whatever. Release the button and it unmutes the mic.

If you are recording remotely (connecting with your co-hosts/guests via the internet), you should be using an ethernet cable rather than Wi-Fi. It is almost always faster and more reliable.

This may seem obvious, but you are going to want comfortable chairs. You might be sitting there for hours and you don't want to be shifting uncomfortably the whole time.

Perhaps the most important piece of hardware you can have . . . a beverage. Podcasting is just a whole lot of talking, my friends, and your mouth is going to get dry. Have a beverage handy—sip away!

Software

WITH GRIFFIN MCELROY

One of the biggest misconceptions about podcasting I frequently hear is that the technical aspects of pod-making are the big roadblocks. Talking for an hour with your buddies? That's easy. You do that all the time. But when it comes to making the computer hear your talking, generating a good-sounding file, and then getting other people to hear that talking? Now that's hard.

The inverse, in my experience, has always been true: once you scale the extremely scalable technical learning curve, working with software is a breeze. It is much, much simpler than being entertaining for an extended period of time, and also, you can eat snacks while you're doing it (which you really shouldn't be doing while recording, because yuck).

Unless it's an ASMR podcast!

Actually Trav, I checked, and still, yuck.

Before breaking down the types of software you're going to need in order to put together your podcast, I think it's helpful to look at the goals you're trying to accomplish with said applications. To get your mouth sounds into a computer brain and then onto the internet, you're going to need:

- A way to record audio on your computer
- A way to edit audio files together
- A way to talk to remote guests or cohosts, if necessary
- A way to record backups of remote calls
- A way to make audio files sound better
- A way to create music for your show, if necessary
- A way to input the metadata (i.e., episode number, author, thumbnail image) on your finished audio file
- A way to upload your show to your hosting service

If you're starting from scratch here, I'd be willing to bet you could solve a couple of those right now. You probably use Skype, Discord, Zoom, or some other VoIP (Voice over Internet

Protocol) software to chat with remote friends; there is a bevy of serviceable options for chatting with distant cohosts. You can upload your show using any ol' internet browser once you have a platform that can host your audio files—a whole 'nother kettle of fish that we'll get into later in the book.

That's good news #1. Good news #2: most of those requirements can be handled by a single application. One piece of software designed to streamline every part of the audio creation process. One executable to rule them all, and in the darkness bind them.

Your Digital Audio Workstation

I adore this terminology, because it sounds so overtly professional for the work I've often done with it. Oh, what software did I use to cut together this audio of three grown men talking about sexual Garfield fan art? My *digital audio workstation*. The episode where I ate, like, forty pizza rolls in nearly as many minutes? Well, that's another opus *lovingly* crafted on my digital audio workstation.

As far as I can tell, any piece of software that allows you to manipulate audio files to create newer, better audio files counts as a digital audio workstation, or DAW. As you might imagine, it's a pretty broad umbrella, as the term "audio" covers, well, a lot of stuff, obviously. Music, podcasting, narrative fiction, news reporting, atmospheric soundscapes—there are DAWs that are more targeted for each of those specific purposes.

For podcasting, I'd recommend going with a DAW that's designed for spoken word content rather than the more musical end of things—though, really, it all comes down to user preference. I know plenty of producers who use Logic Pro X, Apple's music-making software, to edit their podcasts.

Those three pieces of software—a VoIP, a DAW, and a browser—are really all you need to make a podcast. If you're looking to go a little more high-touch, you can add music or really master your audio using external specialty tools. I'll provide some recommendations later in this section.

But before you go any further in this book, you'll need a basic understanding of **what recording a podcast actually looks like**. Computationally speaking. Physically speaking, in our case, it looks like a tired man wearing gym shorts, looming over his desk with unspeakably bad posture. You don't need to emulate that. *You should not emulate that.*

The Digital Audio Workstation and You

Welcome to the most controversial section in this entire book. The software I use to make our podcasts, from single-track episodes of *Wonderful!* to thirty-track, highly produced *Adventure Zone* finales, is Audacity, an open-source, completely free DAW that I've been using for a decade now.

My brothers *despise* me for this fact. They harbor an open, profound hostility toward me because of my choice in DAW. I'm sure there's some kind of sidebar here with one or both of them sounding off about how Audacity is unreliable, and their shit is so much better, and they don't know why I was assigned to write this section of the book.

Fucking Audacity. Lemme ask you a question: How many times would a DAW have to crash, consuming your show and hours of work and shitting it into the obsidian nothingness, before you'd invest the literal *minutes* it would take you to learn new software? One? Two? A dozen? I'm seriously asking, because my little brother seems to have *no discernible ceiling*. I beg you to learn REAPER. It's, like, $60 and there's a generous free trial.

Audacity is a monster that has eaten my recordings in front of my face while I cried literal tears. I would *never* use it to record ever again. That said, I do use it for editing because it's very user friendly.

I don't think we're allowed to do sidebars in our own sections, but I edit all the shows we do together, and I've only ever really lost, like, one file in more than ten years of doing podcasts. My brothers are actual babies.

Here's the thing: Audacity is completely free, is really easy to start using, and has a nice, high skill ceiling for anyone looking to improve the quality of their audio work. You can easily pick it up, make some stuff, edit it, and export it for publishing like *that*, and as time goes on, if you want to get more detailed with your work, there's plenty of stuff under the hood for you to learn how to mess with.

In short: it's perfect for an amateur podcaster.

The best part about Audacity is that it can teach you the ins and outs of what you need out of a DAW with very little friction. If you find Audacity not to your liking, you'll have that general knowledge of how DAWs work and what you prefer, which will make it that much easier to find your weapon of choice. I guess you could say it's a gateway drug. Except for me. I still get very, very high on Audacity several times a week.

You're going to be using your DAW for two distinct purposes: for **recording** and then for **editing**. Always in that order. (Please don't try to edit audio you haven't recorded yet, because that would mean you've slipped loose from the time-field and now somebody has to come get you.) We're going to cross those two respective bridges when we get to them—for right now, it would be useful for you to have a basic understanding of how a DAW accomplishes those goals. I'm going to give a quick rundown on Audacity; if you're at home, willing, and able, you may want to go ahead and download it yourself. It's free, and it works on Windows, Mac, and Linux.

If you're playing the home version of our game, I'll give you a minute to finish the installation.

Okay, let's proceed.

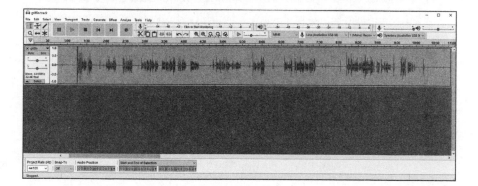

It's beautiful.

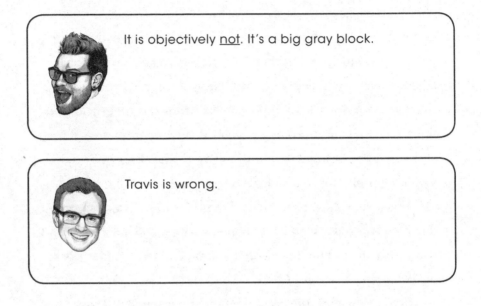

It is objectively <u>not</u>. It's a big gray block.

Travis is wrong.

If you're at all acquainted with any kind of media-editing software, that layout should look somewhat familiar to you. At the top, you've got all the tools you'll need to move around the tracks you record, monitor them in real time, or manipulate them however you need. Below that is a single track in the project timeline, filled with my mellifluous voice, as represented by those sound waves. The menu bar at the top of the screen contains all the other functions of the software—effects, file management, etc.

The basic workflow of Audacity is fairly simple. After making sure your recording settings are on point—selecting the correct microphone, number of recording channels, and so on— you'll record your audio. After you stop recording, you'll have your one big chunk of raw audio that you can trim, apply effects to, or mix with other clips and tracks as your projects get more sophisticated.

Still, there's probably some unfamiliar stuff on that screen, so let's run through that real quick. (It's okay if you don't remember all this stuff; we'll be dipping back into Audacity in later chapters, when it comes time to actually use it.)

We have our **Tools Toolbar (1)**, which, yes, is a bit redundant. It speaks to the ease of use of Audacity that nearly all its main functions can be summarized in these six tools. (Honestly, I only ever use four of them!) These allow you to select sections of audio, adjust your zoom on the track, move clips around the timeline, and adjust volume levels at different points across the timeline.

Next is the **Transport Toolbar (2)**, which should seem pretty familiar to you if you've ever, you know, watched or listened to any media. Pause, Play, Stop, Skip to Beginning, Skip to End, Record. Do you *really* need me to tell you what these buttons do? Shit, y'all. Get it together.

Next we've got two handy tools for making your audio *actually* audible: the **Recording Meter (3a)** and the **Playback Meter (3b)**. The Recording Meter is what you'll use while recording audio to make sure you're coming in at a good level. The Playback Meter is what you'll use while you're editing and mastering your finished track, to make sure you haven't made things too sonically unpleasant with all your ceaseless tinkering.

Below those is the **Device Toolbar (4)**. You can use this to select the microphone and audio output device you'll want to use for the project—or you can pick those through the Preferences menu, accessible (like most other functions of the software) through the menu bar at the top of the screen. You can also use the Device Toolbar to select the number of channels you want to record to, which is a slightly more complicated concept to grasp.

By default, Audacity will have you set to record on one channel, which is called "mono recording." For, like, 99.9 percent of you, you're going to want to leave that there. Think of a

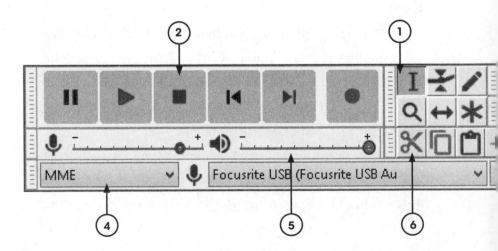

mono recording as being "flat," where all the sounds contained within it are being delivered to the listener in a uniform manner. In stereo, your mic will pick up two channels of recording: left and right. Your voice has depth now. If you record the audio of an entire room—around the table for a board gaming podcast, for instance—you'll simulate the positions of the people speaking.

Now, imagine your listener is riding their bike to work and only has their right earbud in. Everyone on the left side of the room? They sound like ghosts, wailing down the corridors of a very old pirate ship. That's a dramatic example, but it's one of many reasons you shouldn't do your podcast in stereo sound. It's *disquieting* to have the voices you're listening to pinging around in your skull or, worse, to have two cohosts sharing the same mic divided up between earphones. It's a pitfall I've seen a lot of early podcasts fall into, and you can avoid that same fate: keep it mono.

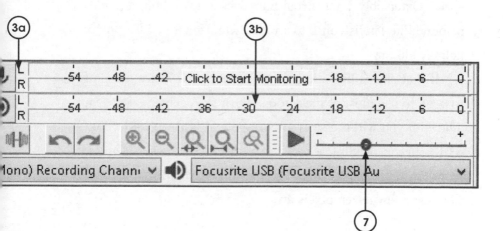

For the record, I do my show *The Empty Bowl* in stereo. I have a stereophonic track of crashing waves that I leave in stereo to give it a kinda cool surround sound effect. But what do I know, I'm just *an artist.*

Moving on from there, we have the **Mixer Toolbar (5)**, where you can adjust your recording and playback volumes; the **Edit Toolbar (6)**, which has a few handy functions that are also mapped to keyboard shortcuts (Cut, Paste, Trim, Silence, etc.); and, finally, the **Play-at-Speed Toolbar (7)**, which lets you listen back to your project at whatever speed you choose.

Confession time: when I'm in a hurry, sometimes I'll edit *My Brother, My Brother and Me* while playing it back at double speed. Ostensibly, I get through it twice as fast, though it makes it sound like I'm listening to a weirdly foul-mouthed Chipmunks holiday album.

If that seems like a lot, let me assure you: you're not going to need to use most of these tools when you're just starting out. The stuff you will use slots into a really logical workflow. You'll find yourself needing a tool for a specific purpose—*how do I move this clip from here to there?*—and then you'll find the solution just a few dozen pixels away.

Some Other Software You Should Know

Your DAW is by far the most important piece of software in your production pipeline, but you'll probably end up using a few others to get your show made.

Here are some that I can think of:

- **Skype, Discord, Slack, or some other VoIP to connect you and your distant cohosts.** Assuming you have remote cohosts, you'll need some way to talk to them. You likely have this figured out. We've used a few over the years, and don't get it twisted: they've all got their little peccadilloes that make them problematic for podcasting purposes. Skype's audio quality isn't great, Discord has a tendency to duck audio when folks cross talk, Slack introduces delays from time to time, and so on. We've recently become big fans of a service called CleanFeed, which offers a browser-based voice chat solution that sounds fairly good—but its biggest selling point is that it also works perfectly as . . .

- **An application for recording your VoIP calls.** Most VoIP apps offer some method of recording *right there* in the app, which is what we do every time we record. This will give you one audio file with everyone talking on it. *This should not be your first choice, if you can help it.* The person recording the file will sound great; their mic is being recorded directly. Everyone else's is going to get chewed up and spit out through the internet's cavernous maw. You'll have *a version* of your conversation saved, and if something goes horribly wrong with one of your cohost's local recordings, you may need it for backup. But the recorded VoIP call will never sound as good as several local recordings edited together. CleanFeed is capable of recording each caller to separate tracks—but only if you're paying for the premium version. It's an improvement, but again, using locally recorded audio should be your goal.

- **External audio processing tools.** Your main editing software will likely include everything you need to get your audio in ship shape, but there's plenty of stand-alone apps that can help streamline the post-production process before you get in too deep. I use an app called Levelator for virtually everything I edit. It's free, and it can be used on Windows, Mac, and Linux. You take a WAV file (the most common audio format we use throughout the production process), drag and drop it into Levelator, and it will process the file and establish smooth, uniform audio levels throughout. It's a shortcut I heavily rely on, and you should too.
- **A DAW for making music for your show, if that's something you're into.** I use Logic Pro X, which is Apple's pro-

fessional music production software, to make all the music for *The Adventure Zone.* If you've got a Mac, you should have free access to GarageBand, which has a metric ton of loops and instruments for you to futz around with, but I don't really have time to provide a tutorial for that here. (You should go goof around with those, though, because they're *rad as hell.*) There's a cornucopia of options for other operating systems as well—Ableton, Pro Tools, FL Studio, you name it. There are massive online communities dedicated to these DAWs, and learning how to use them isn't nearly as difficult as you might think.

- **An application for finalizing your metadata.** Like I mentioned earlier, your finished show will need some baked-in information that can surface for listeners when they listen to it. You know how iTunes tells you the artist behind a song and the name of the album it's on and shows you the cover art of said album? That's all metadata. Audacity will let you set pretty much all of that when you export your file, but I use an app called ID3 Editor to finalize all our episodes, just as a means of double-checking that everything looks good from the listener's end before we publish.

- **An internet browser.** You'll need one to upload your show to your hosting platform, which we'll cover when it's time to talk postproduction.

If I can add one more consideration when you're getting your slate of software ready to go: don't be afraid of this stuff, especially your DAW. Audacity is about as user-friendly as software gets, but even if that weren't true, remember that nobody has to hear everything you create with it.

Record yourself singing some random garbage, then go up to the Effect drop-down menu and get weird with it! Make some shitty harmonies over multiple tracks! Do impressions, and then try to chop and screw them into lo-fi beats. Then delete them! That kind of toy box approach to learning a DAW is an effective—and fun!—way to start gaining experience and confidence with its suite of tools.

Where to Record

WITH JUSTIN MCELROY

You tug on the heavy door of the studio and hear an odd *shwush* as air rushes out of the room. The walls are covered by weird divots, giving the impression of the world's largest egg carton. The lighting is dim but comforting. The chairs? Beyond comfortable. And then there's the strangest bit: the way sound seems to die as soon as it escapes your lips. The team of engineers you've got monitoring your every word gives the nod and presses the Record button. This is a professional studio and . . . you don't have one. (Well, we're assuming you don't have one; it would be weird that you're spending your precious life minutes reading this if you had one of those.)

The good news is that with no more than a few bucks and a little know-how, you can fashion a recording space that'll be *just fine.*

Besides, studios can *smell weird.* Think about how many people have gotten their spit all over those microphones. Trust us, our dad worked in radio for years and the smell still haunts us. (To simulate: find the oldest blanket in your closet and find some old dudes to blow cigarette smoke into it for thirty years. Ugh, pass.)

Less Than Ideal Is Ideal

Even though your own private recording studio isn't realistic, it is a useful metric to work off of.

The dream studio would be:

1. Completely accessible to you at all times
2. Completely silent and impermeable to outside noise
3. Perfectly treated to dampen sound waves (more on that in a second)
4. Perfectly comfortable

You won't be able to meet these ideals (that would be a professional studio, right?), so the trick is trying to get as close as reasonably possible. Imagine those four criteria like little sliders. You want them each to be as high as you can get them. They don't have to be at ten, but if any of them are at zero, you're not going to have much success.

If you have a space that's *usually* accessible to you that's *sort of* insulated from outside noise and *basically* treated to dampen sound waves while still being *kinda* comfortable, you've got an ideal space to start podcasting in.

I'm going to assume that the concept of accessibility is one that needs no further explanation, but let's take the other three factors one at a time.

Secret Pro Shortcut

Sorry, I should have said this earlier, but there's a really easy solution to this whole thing, and if it makes sense for you, I don't wanna waste a bunch of your time. So, here it goes:

Record in a closet, specifically one filled with clothes. That'd be ideal. If you could just shove yourself into a closet and record by yourself (or squeeze in a bunch of your friends), read no further. Just do that.

This is a short-term fix probably (especially since the closet might get a little muggy during a lengthy recording session), but if you just wanna get started immediately, it'll meet most of the criteria, trust me.

Silent but Deadly

There are two different kinds of sound you have to consider when you're recording: the kind you make while recording your show and the preexisting kind. We're gonna talk about the second one *first*, because I'm a *structural rebel* who never learned to play by *The Man's Rules*.

Close your eyes right now and really—oh, crud, you stopped reading. Hmm, I'll wait until you open them again. Okay, so close your eyes—*not yet*—but in a second, close your eyes and really focus on what you hear. See how many different sounds you can isolate.

Welcome back! First, *wasn't that relaxing*? You should really try to do that more often. Second, how many different sounds did you notice? I'm on my porch, so I heard my baby's white noise machine through the window, a car, some birds, the wind in the trees, a distant Weedwacker, and the *Twin Peaks* soundtrack, which I listen to while I write to give my prose the appropriate amounts of melancholy and nostalgia. Any one of these noises could be really bad for a recording, so I would recommend that you not record on my porch. Let's find a more secluded corner of the house, okay?

Small spaces on the top floor are nice, because you're not going to get foot traffic noises from higher floors. Basements are good, unless there are a lot of creaky floorboards above you or the Wi-Fi can't reach. Unless you're on a top floor, it's a good idea to have someone jump up and down and scream right above your recording location to see how much sound leak you can expect into your recording space.

At the very least, your space needs to be behind a closed door so anyone you share your home with (pets included) can go about their lives without messing up your show.

There are less obvious, more insidious noises to be aware of as well. You'll want to shut off any fans in your space. Also, crank up the air-conditioning and listen for a hum or buzz. If it comes through on playback, you'll want to shut it off before you record.

There have been episodes of *My Brother, My Brother and Me* (especially from the early days) that we've had to dispose of because we couldn't be troubled to turn our AC off. Don't be like us, you're better than that.

Processing Audio Complaints

I've actually found listener feedback on audio quality to be one of the most useful tools when troubleshooting your space. Much like you don't notice the smell of your own home, your ears (especially if you're just starting in audio) may have learned to ignore certain sounds. You may no longer hear echoey voices, air-conditioning, pet noises, your children asking you to stop writing your podcasting book long enough to look at their draw-ing they made at school, etc., but your listeners will pick up on it instantly.

Other culprits to look out for: noisy PC or game console fans that you've learned to tune out, space heaters, and aroma-therapy machines that make a bubbling sound that drives your younger brothers absolutely apeshit.

P.S. I'm so fucking sorry that I have an anxiety disor-der and I like a little lavender in the air to help me unwind, *Travis*. Maybe you should find a different brother who's a little less complicated, eh, *Griffin*? What's that, you haven't got another brother? Oh, weird, maybe you should start treating this one *a little nicer* then.

If you're ever in doubt about how much ambient noise is bleeding into your studio, there's only one reliable fix: turn on your microphones, record the room without any speech, and then play it back. You'll probably never get complete silence, and there are some tools you can use after the fact to clean it up, but get it as close as you can.

Intentional Noise

Podcasts are, of course, a creative medium and as such have no actual *rules* per se, even as it pertains to your recording space. Background noise may be very important to providing a sense of place—for example, crickets to convey that you're recording on a quiet, peaceful night.

I would contend that even if the noise is intentional, you'd be better served recording your audio in a silent room and then recording your background noise separately to give you control over how loud those background sounds will be.

Sydnee and I once did an episode of our TV podcast *Satellite Dish* while driving. We thought it would give the whole thing a fun road trip vibe, but the noise of the engine made it almost unlistenable.

These days, I'm smarter. For example, I mentioned my meditative show *The Empty Bowl* earlier, which includes the sound of waves crashing. I keep these background sounds on a separate track so I can lower the volume when I need to.

A Beautiful Pillow Room

Just a warning that I (Justin) am getting way the hell out of my depth here in this section, as it deals with a lot of acoustic science that I barely understand. But listen, you just need to trust me, okay? I'm a professional podcaster, and you've already paid for the book.

Once you've eliminated as much exterior noise as you can, you'll need to control how the sounds you make with your mouth and kazoo (applicable to kazoo-centric shows only) bounce around the room.

Here's the layman's version of this: when you talk you make sound waves. Some of those waves go into the microphone, but some go shooting around the room and bounce off any hard, flat surfaces they can find. Those sound waves are reflected back to your microphone just a nanosecond or so after your initial burst of mouth audio, creating a bunch of very tiny echoes. These sound bad, generally speaking.

Wanna hear a great sample of this effect? Download episode fifty-five of *My Brother, My Brother and Me*. It's one of the only times we ever recorded all in one room outside of a live show. We recorded in our dad's office, and it was completely untreated, so you'll hear some pretty harsh echoes. Why were we all in the same room, you ask? Well, our Mawmaw Lou passed away, and Travis and Griffin were in town for the funeral. And I . . . don't

> know why I just told you that. Let's get back to pod-
> casting.

The solution? Eliminate as many of those hard, flat surfaces as possible. Here are a few possibilities:

1. **Spend a bunch of money on acoustic panels to hang on the walls and ceiling:** Great choice, but pricey. There are cheaper tiles you can buy online in bulk, but I haven't found them to provide much noise dampening.
2. **Build them yourself on the cheap (tutorials are all over YouTube):** Also a good choice, but it's a ton of work, and what if you accidentally staple your fingers to them?
3. **Put a bunch of bookshelves in the room:** This was my strategy for the first few years we made podcasts. Books are fantastic at absorbing sound, and their irregular shapes make them ideal for diffusion.
4. **Moving blankets:** You know, the big boys that you throw on your armoire to keep it from getting dinged up in a move? These are cheap and thick, and you can hang them basically everywhere. They just don't, you know, look *great*.
5. **A rug:** Oh God, look down—what's that giant reflective surface? That's right, your floor. Hey, don't panic! Maybe just toss a rug down there.

6. **Clothes:** Like in a closet? But you better not have a closet you can record in, because then you spent all that time reading this section for nothing.

One solution I wouldn't mess with are mic isolation shields. These are like giant foam binders, and you prop them in front of your face while you record. They block your view of your computer and other people you're recording with, and they're not all that effective to begin with.

The best fix for you is probably some combination of all these treatments. I record in a carpeted room with plenty of bookshelves and acoustic panels that I installed a couple of years ago. It's *still* not perfect, because I have a large desk, computer monitors, and a TV that all reflect sound. But it's pretty good, and that's okay by me.

If you're using a really great directional microphone for podcasting, this may not be that big of an issue, because they're designed to pick up just the mouth sounds as much as possible. But having a well-soundproofed recording space certainly doesn't hurt.

Testing is the answer here: make a recording before you

start fooling with soundproofing. Talk, cry, scream, laugh, whatever, and then play it back and listen. If the echo isn't bothering you, it probably won't bother your listeners.

Getting Comfortable

This isn't the first factor everyone considers when they're picking a studio space, but that's not a surprise. You can live with discomfort, right? Sure, the woodshed you record in is sweltering for half the year and freezing for the other half; sure, its "chairs" are rusty wrought-iron benches and the windows are positioned specifically so the sun can shine directly into your eyes sixteen hours every day. But it's quiet, isn't that enough? Friend, I'm here to tell you it's not.

You're an *artist*, after all, and you can't make your podcast art if you're distracted by how much you'd like to watch your folding chair fall silently into a bottomless well.

 When my wife, Rachel, and I started recording podcasts together, she would sit on a piano bench in my office while I sat in my futuristic, orthopedically optimized Big Boy chair. The discrepancy between our situations was untenable, so I picked up a

padded folding chair from Target—which Justin, upon viciously criticizing me, one-upped with an *even fancier* Big Boy chair he gifted her for her birthday. This is a long way of saying that I am, all things considered, a deeply thoughtless person, cohost, and husband.

That's not to say you should be sitting at all, of course. Ideally you'd be standing. It's better for your health, vocal performance, and energy levels if you stand.

I mean . . . I don't. I don't stand, I sit, and I'm wild about it. But I *should* stand, and you should too. So, comfortable chairs are a must. Just make sure they're not squeaky (for obvious reasons).

Back to temperature. I always have my air-conditioning off when I record, so I run it at full blast right before I record to get the room comfortable.

Good lighting is important too, but that's really more a question of preference. I find overhead light really oppressive, so I tend to rely on lamps or open the blinds during the day.

Clutter is something I wish I'd taken more seriously when I started making podcasts. If your recording area is messy, you're just not going to be in the best headspace for making great stuff. (This obviously doesn't apply to you if you're the kind of total dirtbag who just has to have it filthy. I'm not here to judge.)

Hey, you know, a bit of decoration might be nice. I like to surround myself with things that inspire me creatively, which is why I'll never take down my seven-foot-tall *Borat* poster, no matter how much sound it reflects.

Okay, I could go on and on here, but I'm basically spiraling into home decor advice that I'm wildly unqualified to give. You get the idea.

Every Little Bit

If there's one consistent theme to our podcast advice, it's one of iterative improvement. No one is going to be perfect at the start, because no one is ever perfect. That's absolutely applicable to recording environment.

Are you going to have a perfect home studio from episode one? Probably not. Have there been plenty of successful podcasts that have launched in the exact same scenario? A ton of them.

The key thing is that you've put a bit of thought and energy into making the best recording environment you can reasonably create. From there it's just a matter of making improvements to your space when it makes sense.

And at least *try* standing.

CHAPTER THREE
Let's Record

Okay, so this is the part that is the hardest to write a step-by-step guide for. As cringe-y as it is to say, recording is where the **art of podcasting** happens, and the step by step of making [sigh] **art** can be difficult to nail down. We toyed with writing, "Now just, you know, talk and stuff" in huge letters, but our editor said that would be "a total rip-off" and "kind of lazy, fellas" and "please stop emailing me, I have real books to work on, just write the chapter already."

We can't tell you *how* to record a great, compelling show, because we don't know you and everything that makes you a great and compelling person. This is the cool part, the part where you really make it your own. There is only one expert in making your perfect podcast, and that's *you*. So rather than a how-to, the following sections are more guidelines and best practices that you can try to observe while you're making your show.

We can't show you how to fly, so we're going to whisper inspiration into your ear and then push you off the tallest branch.

Where's Your Head?

WITH JUSTIN MCELROY

Before you sit down to record anything, it's important to do a quick check-in with yourself to make sure you're in the right headspace. Stressed? Sad? Anxious? Tired? Maybe you can reschedule so you give the best possible performance you can.

You won't always have that luxury. Sometimes you have one solitary hour in the whole of the week when you and your co-hosts are able to get free. Other times, recording can help lift you out of a funk. There have been many times when I have felt too stressed to record my meditative cereal podcast, *The Empty Bowl*, but ended the recording session feeling infinitely more chill.

It's important to continue to police your mood while you record. Don't let your mind wander or start poking around online where you could run into potential stressors or distractions. My brothers and I avoid talking about anything business related when we're about to make a show. Silence and hide your phone so your good vibes won't be slaughtered by a reminder that you've got a root canal tomorrow. (See also "Focus" below.)

Sometimes you won't even be the one to realize that you're not in a good headspace (because brains are weird and often bad). I can count more than a couple of times my brothers have pointed out mid-recording that I seemed a little out of it, which prompted me to realize that I actually had been awake with the baby all night and hadn't eaten and wasn't wearing pants.

Sometimes life happens and it means that recording can't, and that's fine. Making podcasts is hard enough without having to struggle with an uncooperative brain. Remember, you are the only judge of whether you're in a position to *make your art.*

Focus

WITH GRIFFIN MCELROY

Podcasts are traditionally recorded on computers, which are often connected to the internet, which is an infinite distraction engine that will one day doom mankind. Keeping your focus on the conversation you're having and *off literally anything else* seems like it should be an easy habit to get into. I literally got distracted by some emails that came in while I was writing that sentence, so let me assure you, keeping focused on your podcast conversation requires a level of discipline that you might not—and may never—fully possess.

The internet isn't the sole thing that can break your focus in the middle of a conversation. Maybe a cool bird flies by outside. Maybe your brain conjures up a memory of that one time a cool bird flew by outside. All it takes is for you to miss a few crucial seconds of your discussion, and you could send the flow of your podcast crashing down around you. Listeners will probably know you weren't really paying attention. Your cohosts, assuming they know you fairly well, will *definitely* know.

If you're easily distracted (which all three of us totally, totally are), do whatever you need to do before you click Record to ensure you can stay dialed in on the task at hand. Before each recording, I close everything on my computer that I'm not actively using for the show and put my phone on the piano bench across the room. We don't use video chat, so by default, I kinda just stare at the grain of my desk and listen as hard as I can. For an hour or two. I now realize this makes me look like a serial killer.

There's a certain amount of *focusing on focusing* that you've gotta do if you want to stay sharp, but the more dialed in you are, the easier it is for you to listen, which makes it easier for you to keep the conversation moving, which makes it—you get the picture.

Remember the Audience

WITH GRIFFIN MCELROY

In Patrick Rothfuss's Kingkiller Chronicle series, which are the best books ever, the protagonist uses a training exercise to increase his Alar—his supernatural mental prowess. In said exercise, the hero divides his mind into different chambers, each actively working through a different idea, question, or memory. In doing so, he's able to think multiple complex thoughts simultaneously, which—I won't spoil it—eventually gives him the power to kill the big evil wizard.

Oh, shit, I spoiled it.

Anyway, I mention this because I realize we've given you a lot to chew on in this chapter, a lot of lessons to keep in mind while doing your show. And I hate to add one more concept onto the pile, but it's one that I think is *vitally* important—and is, in fact, the number one piece of advice I have for folks who want to make a better podcast.

When you're making a podcast, remember that you're

making a podcast that people are going to listen to. Over time, with luck, you'll have a good idea of what those people generally like about you and your show. Once you do, remember you're making a podcast that *those specific* people are going to listen to.

I am in no way suggesting you pander to the people who have shown an interest in your mouth-speaking. Rather, I'm trying to put you in a headspace that will make it easier to realize when your show's going off the rails.

That clumsy transition between segments: Did it seem uncomfortable to you? Did your conversation come off as unnatural and robotic? Did that last segment turn into an exhausting, self-indulgent info dump? Were you and your cohost a little too nasty to each other just now? Have you said something *remotely* entertaining in the last, oh, let's say, ten minutes? Did your cohost just fucking *burp*?

It's easy to write stuff like that off as a little transgression—or, hell, not a transgression at all—when, to your listeners, it's probably enough to send them sailing away from Your Podcast Island out to fairer seas, where the podcast hosts don't burp.

I don't want this line of thinking to give you the yips before you even start, but believe me, it's essential. Nearly every writing instructor I've ever had has advised me to read my first draft aloud before diving into edits, just to give myself a different, external perspective. While you can more easily achieve that perspective during postproduction, keeping it front-of-mind while you're recording is going to make your show just so, so, *so* much better.

Mic Technique

WITH GRIFFIN MCELROY

Y'all remember Tay Zonday? "Chocolate Rain"? Man, that shit was hilarious. Remember the parts of the video where he makes a big point out of leaning away from the mic to breathe? What a funny thing to do, right? What a weirdo, huh?

Actually, you *judgmental butthole,* Tay Zonday was a fucking *master of his craft.*

See, there are lots of wrong ways to talk into a microphone— and I'm not referring to the things you say, but *how* you actually say them with your mouth and body and lungs and stuff. When Mr. Zonday moves away from the mic to breathe, he does so to keep you from hearing him gulp down lungfuls of oxygenated air like some kind of sick farm animal. Instead, you just hear the buttery-rich bass tones you tuned in for.

Okay, fine: you don't have to lean away from the mic every time you breathe. But a big part of mic technique *is* paying attention to your proximity to your microphone and ensuring you're not, like, wheezing directly into it. If you find yourself to be an *enthusiastic* nose breather, having your microphone directly in the path of your nostrils is going to force listeners to hear each and every one of your inhalations and exhalations in unwelcome detail. Since *not breathing* isn't exactly an option, try moving your microphone above the line of nose-fire; or, if your mic has a pickup pattern that supports it, try rotating the mic outward a bit so you speak into it at an angle. I possess a sinus system that some have described as "Kafkaesque," so that's the technique that works for me.

You should also pay *super* careful attention to your plosives, which refers to the harsher letters of the alphabet that you voice by cutting off airflow to the vocal tract. Chief offenders include stop consonants that you create with your tongue (like *k, t, d,* and *g*), but the ones to really watch out for are your lip-based consonants: *p* and *b*. Plosives, particularly *p* and *b*, create little bursts of wind that, taken head-on into a mic, sound terrible. There's equipment you should probably think about acquiring to limit this, like a mesh windscreen or foam pop filter, but you can also limit it with your technique. Just make sure you're delivering those plosives not directly *into* the microphone but, rather, *across* it at a suitable angle.

If you're struggling with this concept, just record an episode and listen to it, paying careful attention to the obnoxious breathing noises and sharp audio pops. Next time you record, you'll hopefully know what to look out for.

Food and Drink

WITH JUSTIN MCELROY

Here are our two rules about eating food on mic:

1. Unless you are doing a podcast specifically about eating food on mic and then reviewing that food, you shouldn't eat while you record.
2. You shouldn't make a podcast about eating food on mic.

It might not bother everyone, but there's a sizable portion of the podcast-listening population who are yucked out beyond all recognition when they hear people eat. It also makes you harder to understand.

If you need another reason not to eat, remember the unspoken contract between podcaster and listener: they are giving up their most precious commodity (life minutes) to listen to your show, so the least you can do is make recording your sole focus while you're in front of a mic. Eating while you record makes it feel like you'd rather be anywhere else.

Beverages are a necessity. Water is obviously the gold standard. It's really important to stay hydrated while you record if you want your best possible sound. We would, of course, be lying if we said we didn't just as often have coffee.

But we wanted to give water a hearty pat on the back. Hooray, water!

Should you drink and record? Unless your show is specifically designed around you being inebriated (and there are many fine programs in that grand tradition), we'd avoid it, at least at first. You're just never going to be as sharp as you would be stone-cold sober, and when you are just getting your footing, you'll need all your wits about you to simultaneously talk, listen, and transition between topics.

We'll have a drink now and then, but it's a very rare (and not so great) live show where we've teetered on the edge of "drunk."

If you feel confident that you're at your most charming when you've got one in you, go for it.

Make sure, especially if you're not recording with your own gear, that any beverages have lids or are kept far away from the equipment. There are plenty of reasons podcasts fail; don't let yours be "because Jeff dumped a room-temperature Wild Cherry Pepsi on my computer."

Recording Persona

WITH TRAVIS MCELROY

All right, dearest reader, I'm gonna put on my director hat and sit in my director's chair while talking to you through my director's megaphone for just a moment. When you sit down at that microphone, I want you to turn on and turn it up. No, not the microphone, you silly goose. I'm talking about your *whole vibe*. A common mistake hosts make is to bring the same energy to recording that they bring to their everyday life. That just isn't going to do it, my friend.

In the next couple of paragraphs, I'm going to say this about a dozen different ways because it is important: **you have to perform.** Even if you are just being yourself, you have to perform. It is the energy difference between telling a story about a weird thing that happened to one friend and telling the story to a roomful of people at a party.

Now, let me be clear: I am not saying you have to be super excited and off-the-wall. It is way more esoteric than that. You need to be more engaging. That might mean high energy, but in my experience it usually means being attentive to whatever I am talking about.

In acting, there is a whole method based around tactics and objectives. I won't go into it here, but suffice it to say that it is all about what you are trying to get from your audience and choosing active ways to do that. Think about the difference between the tactic "to talk" and "to fascinate," "to thrill," or "to inspire." The former is bland and passive, while the latter three are all active and will yield far better results. When you sit down to record, think about what you want from your audience and what your active tactics are going to be to achieve said objective.

No matter what kind of podcast you're making, you're really performing every time you record. Your listeners are your audience, and you want to be sure that you're being interesting enough to listen to. Take the time to think about your audience, the vibe you want to give off and what you want them to feel, and get into character, even if that character is just you getting amped talking about training videos.

Think about it this way: Do you think everyone who gives a TED Talk also talks like that in their everyday life? Nope! When they walk out on that stage, they turn it on. So, find out what that means for you and turn it up/on.

What to Talk About

WITH TRAVIS MCELROY

The time has come. Creative energy crackles in the air around you. You sit down to make magic, hit Record, and . . . you can't think of one interesting thing to say.

Do not panic, it happens to everyone. We have been podcasting for a decade, and we run into this just about every episode of *My Brother, My Brother and Me* when it comes to the intro. There's usually about ten minutes of discussion before we hit on something worth saying. So that's lesson one: **It's not live, so you can take a minute to talk (even if it's just out loud to yourself) about where to start.**

There are a few ways to tackle this. First, let's figure out what to talk about if your show is about a specific subject. This applies to shows in which you might review a movie (good or bad), educate the audience about one topic per episode, or discuss current events. **A good place to start is to have a set of criteria that the topic has to meet to be right for your show.** For example, on my wife's and my etiquette podcast, *Shmanners*, the topic at hand has to have some kind of historical significance, to still apply to culture today, and to have some kind of process to follow that we can explain or actionable advice on the subject we can give. We obviously make exceptions when we do biographical episodes, but having these guidelines to follow means we are able to know right away if a possible topic fits the show.

Also, this may seem obvious, but **pick a topic that you are interested in**. I could argue that there is nothing more boring than listening to someone dispassionately talk about a subject I love very much. I once heard a podcast about *Twin Peaks* that started with the host saying, "Well, you all said you wanted us to talk about *Twin Peaks*, so I guess we're going to." I turned it off and never looked back.

Okay, now the second branch of our Choose Your Own Adventure: improv shows. This doesn't have to mean comedy; it just means a show in which you have not prepared what to talk about ahead of time. This can seem really intimidating, but for reasons we will discuss in a moment (see "You Can Edit" on p. 119), it's not nearly as scary as it seems. The hardest part is to separate your mind into two levels, much like we'll talk about in the "Listening" section (p. 115). Level one is doing the talking and is focused on saying interesting stuff. Level two is keeping track of how everything is going analytically and is looking for the next thing to talk about. I tend to think of it in terms of swinging on ropes: **you always have to be ready to grab the next rope**. If the next interesting thing pops up, you have to be ready to let go of the old one and move on. Trust yourself to hold on and keep the conversation going. It is a skill that you will keep getting better at the more you do it.

One last thing: being funny. I'm going to paraphrase something I learned in theater school thanks to an old Russian guy named Stanislavski: **if your goal is to *be* funny, you will always fail.** Being funny is an inactive and amorphous goal. What does that mean? It is completely subjective, and thus impossible to know when (and if) you have achieved it. Instead, focus on active goals. When we record *My Brother, My Brother and Me*, I am trying to make my brothers laugh or to surprise them, impress them, whatever else I can think of. Your goals should be outwardly focused. You should always be trying to get some kind of reaction from your cohosts or the audience. Which brings us to . . .

"Yes, Anding"

WITH TRAVIS MCELROY

You may associate the phrase "yes, and" solely with improv, but it actually can be applied as a skill to every conversation (recorded or in person). "Yes, anding" is a momentum builder that is essential, and the good news is that you are probably already practicing it regularly without knowing it!

"Yes, anding" does not always mean literally saying "yes, and." It is a shorthand way to describe buying into the topic at hand and then contributing to it to keep it going. For example:

> **COHOST 1:** I would argue that *Incredibles 2* is the best Pixar movie.
>
> **COHOST 2:** *Incredibles 2* is good, but the winner is obviously *Wall-E* by far!

Even though they are disagreeing, what Cohost 2 is really saying here is "Yes, this is an interesting topic of conversation,

113

and here is my opinion so that we can continue said conversation." Cohost 2 could have also agreed and then offered justifications. Or Cohost 2 could have simply asked Cohost 1 to justify their position. Anything that helps the conversation build momentum is good "yes, anding."

If Cohost 2 had said, "Yes, it is, and now let's talk about sandwiches," they would have said the *words* "yes, and," but actually they would be denying the topic that Cohost 1 had proposed and offered no new information to the conversation.

Okay, are you ready for the twist? **You don't need to always "yes, and" to keep the conversation going.** To return to the ropes metaphor, if you see your cohost reaching for a frayed rope or a rope that leads to a dead end, sometimes the right thing to do is **"no, but."** For example:

Cohost 1 and 2 have been discussing *The Great British Bake Off* when Cohost 1 says . . .

> **COHOST 1:** Speaking of Noel Fielding, did you ever watch *The Mighty Boosh*? Wanna do a crimp?!
>
> **COHOST 2:** Maybe as bonus content for our patrons, but right now the only crimping I want to talk about is on the edge of a piecrust.

In this example, Cohost 2 has made the decision to stick to the subject at hand. Now, if Cohost 1 feels strongly about the tangent, they could always push back. However, a lot of cohosting is about trust. Think of it like a catcher signaling for a pitch and the pitcher shaking it off. It's not that the topic is "bad"; it's just not the right time for it.

"Yes, anding" and "no, buting" are just two examples of conversational skills that you can utilize in your podcast to keep the energy going. Don't worry if it feels a little clunky at first. The more you practice, the better you'll get!

Listening

WITH JUSTIN MCELROY

If you're recording a show with one or more people, you will be driven by a primal desire to say better, smarter, and funnier things than everyone else at the table. This is human! And it's not even a bad impulse necessarily, but it needs to be balanced with the equally important skill of actively listening to your cohosts.

Think of it in terms of the end product. Your listeners are going to be following the flow of a conversation, and if your ideas don't build off the ideas they've heard directly before, it's going to be a jarring experience.

Of course, if you wait until your turn to talk to think of what to say next, you're less likely to have a cogent, well-conceived thought or joke you can share. This is what breeds awkward silences, which aren't a massive problem because you have the power of editing, but it'd be ideal to avoid them to keep from breaking the flow.

The art of recording with other people is simultaneously listening with the front of your brain while the back of your brain tries to build your next contribution to the conversation. That's not anatomically correct, of course, but we don't want to bore you with the technical jargon we've accrued from our years of intensive study of neurobiology.

The front part of your brain, then, should be preoccupied with listening to, processing, and responding to the contributions of your cohosts. That's the part of your brain that's an audience surrogate, hearing the jokes and pondering the ideas. If the front brain hits upon something you might be able to build on, it should pass it on to the back brain for further processing.

Physical Listening

The front brain should also, incidentally, ensure that you're physically demonstrating active listening (smiles, nods, etc.). There's nothing that can kill your cohost's confidence and energy like your thousand-yard stare. I find that this is even helpful when I'm recording with people remotely, as your physical actions can often force your brain into behaving. If you don't believe me, try smiling for the next five minutes and see if you don't feel a little happier.

It's the back brain's job to process the ideas being sent over by the front brain and build your next contribution. Even if you know exactly what you want to say next, you should keep the flow between the two brain halves going. You never know when a cohost might say something that will spark a better idea or help you solidify a loose thought.

It's tough knowing the right moment to speak, but paying attention to the rhythms of your cohosts is absolutely crucial. A few obvious and not-so-obvious cues:

- You've just been directly asked a question. (This is an easy one.)
- You can feel the flow of the conversation moving away from the point where your contribution would be relevant. This can be jarring, but if you have a really significant point, it's worth pulling the car over. It can be helpful to provide a nicety like "If I could just circle back to something you

said . . ." or what have you. This lets the listener know that you're aware that you're changing direction, but you're doing so thoughtfully.

- You can feel your cohost running out of steam. I know my brothers really well at this point, and I can usually tell when they're building to a good punch line and when they're vamping in the hopes that someone else will step in.
- There's a lull in the conversation. Even if your idea isn't fully formed yet, I think it's okay to jump into a quiet space and just start building the thought as you go. Not ideal maybe, but not usually unpleasant to listen to.

A trickier, though important, move is interrupting with *intention*. This is tough, but if the conversation merits it, I think it's entirely appropriate to intentionally burst into your cohost's flow if doing so can raise the stakes in a satisfying way.

For example, in *My Brother, My Brother and Me*, Travis or Griffin will often say something outlandish, and when I challenge them on it, they'll either double down or immediately retreat—either one can be really funny. The key differentiator here is that I'm not taking the steering wheel away, I'm briefly jerking the wheel so that we careen into . . . I don't know, a rubber chicken factory. Something funny. You get the idea.

Oh man! "A rubber chicken factory"?! Is someone writing this down, because it is comedy gold!

You Can Edit

WITH TRAVIS MCELROY

Are you ready to learn about a podcasting superpower you never knew you had? *You can edit!* This is, no exaggeration, the most important thing you will learn from this book. As long as you are not doing your podcast live (a thing I have not heard of and would call "radio" instead of podcast), you have the ability to completely reshape your podcast as you see fit. In the next chapter, we'll talk about how to edit. Right now it is just important that you remember that you can!

How can you utilize this amazing power to its full potential? For one thing, you can let it take the pressure off. Don't spend your whole recording session overanalyzing the thing you already said. If it's bad, you can cut it later. Focus on what you are currently saying and what you are about to say.

Have some kind of annoying sound pop up during recording?

For me, it's usually my dogs barking. It might also be someone ringing your doorbell over and over, a fire truck driving by with its siren on, your neighbor vacuuming upstairs, and on and on and on. Well, it doesn't need to show up in your audio! Call "hold," take care of it or wait for it to pass, and then resume recording!

Next, and this can be a tough one to get used to, but don't be afraid to halt the whole discussion to talk to your cohosts. We call this talking "off mic." It feels weird saying, "Wait, stop," in the middle of recording, but it really can be the best option sometimes. Does it feel like everything is getting off track and you can't see a way to get it back? Discuss it with your cohosts, edit out the conversation, and keep right on going. Did you move to a new conversation topic that you quickly realized is going nowhere? Stop, jump back, start a new topic, and edit out the false start later!

Not only is talking off mic a good way to quality control, but it can be an essential tool for maintaining healthy relation-ships. Sometimes, things get heated in conversations and people argue. It doesn't even have to be that obvious. Maybe everybody just seems kind of tense or unhappy or whatever. Stop and talk about it. Even if working through the issue completely devours the session and you end up having to record another time, you'll be glad you did.

What else does the power of editing offer you? Well, how

about this: you don't need to fill time. Occasionally, you'll need to look up some piece of information, or a cohost will need to run and grab something, or a thousand other situations resulting in dead air. Sometimes you might have something incredibly witty and interesting to say, but if you don't, then just leave it as silence and cut it later! No one will ever know!

You can also take a second pass at a flubbed line, even nonscripted ones! I'm really bad with names, so sometimes it takes me a couple of tries before I land on a pronunciation I am happy with. I also have a tendency to read one word as another word if I'm going too fast. If either of those happens, don't worry! Just edit out the flub!

Ending the Episode

WITH TRAVIS MCELROY

The hardest thing in love and podcasting is knowing when to walk away. Wow, that's a really great sentence I just came up with. I'm going to put that on a bumper sticker. Anyway, it's time to end your episode.

Here's what *not* to do. Don't spend the last five minutes struggling to think of something else to say. If your episodes are usually forty-five minutes long and this one is only forty, that is totally okay. A slightly shorter episode is way better than an episode that ends with you scooping up the dregs from the bottom of the conversational barrel.

In fact, I would argue that it is better to end the episode *before* you run out of things to say. Hopefully, I'm not the first person to tell you this, but leave them wanting more. Why? Well, there are a couple of really good reasons!

One, when the conversation is clearly done but you are still talking, listeners are likely to go ahead and stop listening to the episode. So, if you have any important announcements or interesting information at the end of the show, you might as well just shout them straight into the garbage can.

Two, these days it's all about binge-listening! I never listen to just one episode of anything. When one finishes, I'm right on to the next. However, if the energy of the episode I'm listening to hits zero, I'm way less likely to pick up with the next. Leave some gas in the tank to get them to the next station!

It's a bit of a shortcut, but this is why I like having a rough goal for episode length. For *Shmanners,* we always aim for between thirty and forty minutes. So, if we have hit that thirty-minute mark and if it feels like we have covered the topic well, we can safely wrap it up!

Also, don't forget what we said about editing. You should feel free to take a second to discuss with your cohosts off mic (you'll edit it out later) about whether they think it's time to wrap up. They may have some real bangers to throw out before you finish.

When it's time to shut it down, don't forget your outro. Mention things like where the audience can find you on social media, any input/feedback you are looking for from the audience, and the importance of sharing the show with friends. Also, be sure to credit anyone you need to credit for stuff contributed to your show. Anyone who has listened to my shows will know that I am a big fan of taglines to close out an episode. So, as always, catch you on the flip side, turkeys.

There they are, all of our recording secrets. Now you know everything! Wait, did we mention that you should make it good? That seems like a pretty important thing. Make your show good, not bad. Okay, that should be everything.

CHAPTER FOUR
Now Let's Make It Listenable

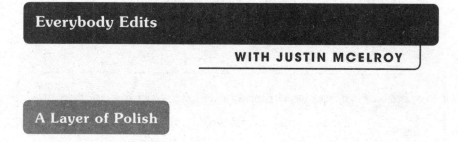

Everybody Edits

WITH JUSTIN MCELROY

A Layer of Polish

With any luck, at this point, you've made a recording that you're happy with and now you're ready to start polishing it up. If not, back up and take another pass. We promised in the last chapter that we'd teach you how to edit to fix your mistakes, and now's the time to do so. But keep in mind: while we've used editing plenty of times to turn a good episode into a very good one, we've not once been able to transform a dud into gold in the DAW. (You remember, right? Digital audio workstation? Of course you do.)

Yes, I said *we've* used editing. While it's true that Griffin edits *My Brother, My Brother and Me* and Travis now handles *The Adventure Zone*, I still produce *Sawbones*, and besides, I taught them both *everything* they know.

The very most important, number one thing that you need to do before anything else, and we really can't emphasize this enough: save your raw file as soon as you record it and hide it away. You want the freedom to experiment with your audio, but if you accidentally make it into a fart with all your machinations, you'll want to be able to start again from scratch.

Is it safe? Is it safe? Okay, great, let's move on.

If you were planning on skipping this section because your divine work doesn't require second-guessing of any kind—don't! Editing is how middling recordings turn out good and good recordings turn out amazing. Knowing that you have that card in your back pocket relieves *so* much pressure from the act of recording. Even if you feel like you're putting up bricks, nothing has to hit the airwaves that you don't want to.

A Brief Note

There are (basically) two different ways you can put your show together. There are obviously dozens of different subcategories within these two, but for reasons that will become immediately apparent, this bifurcation is a useful jumping-off point.

- **The hard shows:** These are your *Serial*s, your Gimlet shows, your *Radiolab*s. Their creators pull together audio from a bunch of disparate sources and then use storytelling prowess, dozens of hours of editing, and a lifetime of broadcasting experience to build a compelling narrative that'll leave the listener spellbound.
- **Shows we know how to make:** You know, boner shows for ding-dongs. People talking a bunch and then stopping after, like, an hour.

Listen, if you were hoping to read a book about podcasting that would somehow teach you how to instantly have a master's degree in broadcasting from a top-tier college and an entry-level gig keeping bullies from throwing Ira Glass's wallet down gutters, we've got bad news: you picked up the wrong book.

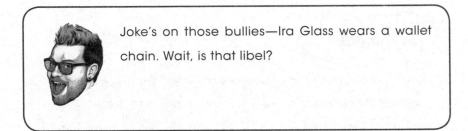

Joke's on those bullies—Ira Glass wears a wallet chain. Wait, is that libel?

Exhaustively reported and finely edited shows like *Serial, This American Life, Reply All*, etc., are really hard to make and require years of professional training and audio tools we don't have and . . . well, we just can't help you there. Okay? If you make a show like those, though, please email us so we can listen to it.

Now that you understand our limitations (soon to be *your* limitations!), let's get to work.

Making Your Masterpiece

In an ideal world, you won't do your editing in a single pass but rather multiple passes with increasing levels of refinement.

We're not sculptors, but it's basically exactly like making Michelangelo's *David*.

So first things first, you need to cut out the parts you don't want anybody to ever hear, stuff that's not for public consumption. If we're making *David*, this is the part where we chip off the plaque attached to our stone that reads PROPERTY OF DAVE'S GIANT MARBLE CHUNK EMPORIUM—DO NOT CARVE—IF FOUND, PLEASE CALL XVI–VIIV.

If you left the mics running when you went to the bathroom, if you said something embarrassing that you wouldn't want anyone to hear, if you had a funny bit that included your Social Security number, cut those bits out now.

If you were marking obvious edit points in your recording track with a dog training clicker or silent pauses like we suggested, these obvious warts would likely be the ones you've already marked for removal. (Cut the dog clicks and silences now too, by the way.)

Once in a great while, we've been able to find a use for these off-mic bits. Once our Nonnee barged in on our dad while he was recording, and he talked to her about French onion soup, and it was perfect for the episode, so we left it in. If you think something might be useful at some point, pull it into a separate file or track on your DAW rather than delete it. Eventually, you'll have hours' worth and you can take a week off by posting a "Too Hot 4 Podcasting" episode of bloopers and outtakes. You're welcome.

The Content Pass

Next, you have to figure out what you want to keep and how to weave those strands into a cohesive listening experience. We're chipping out arms and legs and a head and maybe just the hint of a crotch. It looks like a human, but not *David.*

The best possible way to do this is also the most time consuming. Listen through the entire thing and note the edits you want to make with markers in your DAW or by writing down time codes on paper. Why not just make the edits as you go? Well, you can, but there's always a chance that you've referenced those bits later in the show and that you could lose the listener if they've been cut. We can't tell you the number of times we had an unfunny fifteen seconds that we cut only to find that we built a solid two minutes on top of that moment later in the show that we also had to cut, which spiraled into half the show, until we eventually just went and put the bad fifteen seconds back in. Editing is always easier (and in the end faster) when you know exactly what you have to work with.

The good news is that over time you'll get a better grasp of editing "in the moment." It's better to say, "Wait, let me go back," than try to make something work for twenty minutes, only to have to spend hours editing around it later.

The rigorousness of your edit depends on what kind of thing you want to create. Let's say you're pulling out only the best bits, trying to reduce an hour of audio into a tight twenty minutes. In that case, it's probably more useful to pull the choice clips that definitely work into a separate track until you have something that approximates a show. (This is the way I edit *The McElroy Brothers Will Be in "Trolls World Tour,"* which is sort of a parody of those very good shows I don't know how to make.)

If you want something more conversational, you should be looking for things to remove that break the flow. Leaving in the occasional diversion or tangent might be okay—you just don't want it to derail the show entirely.

It can be helpful to leave large spaces between big chunks of good audio, to help you keep track of what you have to work with. Most DAWs will allow you to glue those functional segments together, maybe even label or color-code them, all of which can make it much easier to put together a final product.

If you get lost in the weeds here, this is useful: remind yourself that in putting out a podcast, you're asking listeners for their most valuable resource—minutes of their life that they will never get back. A lot of pressure, right? It is! But it's also a useful way to think about editing. If the answer to "Is this five minutes of material worth five minutes of someone's life?" is

"No!" then cut it. Editing out our cruft is, in a sense, a moral act and a way of showing your listeners you value them.

The Polishing Pass

The intensity of this last step will vary from show to show and may, indeed, evolve for your show over the years. You can spend hours making your piece pristine and museum-worthy, or you, like us most of the time, can tape a sign to your horrific rock man that says THIS IS DAVID. It's your call.

The occasional chair creaking isn't a big deal on a conversational show like *My Brother, My Brother and Me*. Hell, if it's loud enough, we might be able to milk five minutes of material out of giving the offender guff for it. It wouldn't work as well on a more focused show like *Sawbones* that's a little more buttoned down and educational in tone.

The one bit of polish you almost certainly want to do is remove any evidence that you've made edits. There are certainly tons of articles explaining how to do this scientifically, but the best method we've found is just listening. Our inflection tends to rise and fall in patterns, and if you cut something mid-sentence, it'll often just *feel* off. The solution (sadly) is that you'll probably have to trim more than you want to avoid it sounding clunky.

You can insert cross-fades to mitigate some of the weirdness. The cross-fade basically lowers the volume on the first clip of sound while raising the volume on the second clip to create something that sounds more natural. Your DAW can almost certainly do this automatically.

All this stuff is hard to communicate with text or pictures of waveforms, but trust us, when you listen to your track, you'll know exactly what a bad edit point sounds like. Cut it out or cut around it until it sounds right.

Making these adjustments can feel fiddly, but there's nothing more distracting than noticeable editing. Immediately, the listener starts thinking about what they might be missing, distracting them from whatever great joke you just made about millennial wolfmen or whatever.

A more intense version of the polishing pass includes cutting all or some filler words such as "like" or "um." Even if you don't notice them in your day-to-day speech, these things will drive you crazy once you start looking for them. If you want something that sounds more professional, and you don't mind the work, you may want to nix them.

It's worth noting that all the "likes" and "ums" aren't always deadweight; they're often communicating something. For example, maybe you're unsure of exactly what you're trying to get across, and the "um" is communicating a certain hesitance. That may not be how you want to come across in every episode, but a little bit of filler is part of how most people speak naturally, and doing away with all of those little verbal quirks can shed a little bit of humanity or intimacy in the process.

I would say the same for silence. While you can generally cut it, sometimes silence really makes a moment *land*. Like if one of your brothers has just said something profound about mangoes. Sitting in silence can drive home how amazing it was.

It's Your *David*

The important thing about editing your show is remembering that it is, in fact, *your* show. Other than sloppy edits or leaving in the bit where your racist uncle barged into your office and started spouting his extremely unpalatable theories, there's not really a wrong way to do this.

You know the show you want to make and how natural or professional you want it to sound, or if you don't know already, you will once you've spent some time editing. You may not have the expertise to achieve that. Hell, you may just not have the *time*. (This stuff is a lot of work for *probably* zero money at first.) The important thing is that you keep tinkering until you can release something that you're proud of.

We could bloviate all day about this, but there's really just no substitute for hopping into your DAW and messing around with some audio until you're totally comfortable. Record yourself reading the mail, listen for hiccups, and edit them out. If it sounds weird after your edit, undo your changes and try again. You'll get there. Hell, if we did it, you certainly can.

Music

WITH GRIFFIN MCELROY

I'd like to formally welcome you to the section of the book where we are, without argument, the furthest from our area of expertise that we can get. If it were possible for a book to include a second, smaller book written by a more qualified person, tucked inside the larger book like a secret gun in a hollowed-out Bible, I would almost certainly do that here.

 If it were me, I'd hide the gun in a hollowed-out book about guns so I wouldn't lose it.

Music is an essential part of every podcast, in the sense that every podcast I've ever heard has music in it at some point. At the same time, sourcing that music can potentially be a tricky process, depending on the rights reserved on the song used and the nature of how the podcast uses it.

What makes for good music for your podcast's purposes is completely subjective. You might like completely different styles of music from what I like or your audience does. Not every song you like is going to be compatible with the show you're hoping to produce.

You can see what a kettle of fish this section is to write—I can't tell you what music is good, and I also can't tell you the ins and outs of copyright law (spoiler alert: I am not a copyright lawyer). I super can't do that last part, because you might be a cop. If you're a cop, you legally have to tell me or else it's entrapment.

Instead, I can break down the two main questions you have to answer when considering the use of music in your new, chart-topping podcast: How do you find music, and what's the best way to use it?

Sourcing Music for Your Podcast

I have good news and bad news. First, the bad. You're not going to be able to legally use Coldplay's "Viva La Vida" as your podcast's theme song. I'm sorry for being so blunt, but there's no point dancing around the subject. Unless your uncle works for Coldplay and can get you in a room with Chris Martin, or you saved Chris Martin from a burning building and he owes you a life debt or something—it's not going to happen. Banish the thought.

It's a natural instinct to hear a piece of popular music and envision its use as a theme song or background dressing for a dramatic scene, but the fact of the matter is that popular music is almost certainly going to be out of your podcast's reach. Most music from major recording artists with label representation has the shit copyrighted out of it, and it would likely be exorbitantly expensive for you to use legally.

Now, the good news: there are a lot of other ways of finding music for your show! You might not get that first song you wanted, but the great thing about music is that there is so much of it, and a lot of it is far more accessible than Coldplay's body of work.

Double good news! People already have a lot of memories attached to super well-known songs. Finding a lesser-known song will allow people to associate it with memories of your show!

Here are four ways of finding music for your show, all of which are methods we've used for our podcasts in the past.

You can, if you have the means, **license a copyrighted song**. Yes, I know what I just said—licensing the work of a huge band like Coldplay or the Beatles is going to cost a buck-wild amount of cash, but smaller acts may be able to offer a more affordable agreement. There are a few major music license database websites you could peruse for inspiration—places like Machinimasound and Musicbed have fairly affordable licenses for bespoke tunes. You could also reach out to a musical act via a publicly accessible contact page or its label and find out how much a license for its work would cost you. Just keep in mind that amount is going to fluctuate depending on the popularity of the song and the nature of how you want to use it. Is it for a single episode? For a theme song? For a season? For life?

The less legally sound method of approaching the above is to **just obtain written permission to use a song in your podcast**. Maybe your friend is in a band, and they tell you it's cool for you to use one of their songs. Maybe you reach out to an indie artist you love, and they tell you over email it's no sweat. You're more than likely in the clear to use it as permitted, but keep in mind that this provides you with very little legal ass-covering in the grand scheme of things. (Also, artists deserve compensation for their work. We weren't respectful enough of this fact when we started, but it's totally true. Whatever you can do to support the artist who has chosen to support you isn't just going to be appreciated, it's the necessary gesture to keep this great *wheel of art* a-spinnin'.)

Here's an interesting tidbit that may surprise you: Even if you can get a recording artist to give you permission to use their music in your show, they may not actually have the right to do that. Rights to use music commercially are retained by publishing companies, and they can (and probably will) still scream at you even if your pal Robbie Williams granted you the rights to use "Let Me Entertain You" in a tweet. Anyway, make sure you get the right people to sign off.

One great way to fill your podcast with beautiful, professional-sounding music is to **source it from a collection of Creative Commons works**. A Creative Commons license allows you to use creative works for free, provided you follow whatever stipulations each artist requires for said usage. Maybe it's attribution for the original artist, or maybe it's that you don't include their work in a commercial product. These stipulations are super easy to adhere to and open up so many options for you to explore. CreativeCommons.org has a fantastic list of websites chock-full of music you can use; the Free Music Archive and ccMixter are also great resources. YouTube has a really extensive library as well.

Finally, **you can make music your own damn self!** It's legally sound, it doesn't require you to get permission or follow anyone else's licensing terms, it doesn't cost you a penny, and it gives you access to the infinite symphonies swimming around your dome, just itching to break free. Don't know how to make music? That is, of course, a bottleneck. But there are lots of DAWs (like GarageBand, which comes free on Macs and iOS devices) that include premade loops that anyone can experiment with and cobble together into a song. And hey, maybe while doing so, you'll learn what makes a composition good and pick up some skills that will help you create a song from scratch! Just look up some YouTube tutorials and start poking around!

There are so many ways to find a good song for your podcast, but the best piece of advice I can give you is to stay flexible while hunting for that one ideal track. Don't get your heart set on a song, only to find out its license is unavailable or exorbitantly expensive. Really hunt around until you find the perfect music—in terms of both its fit for your show and its accessibility to you, a responsible, law-abiding podcast creator.

Using Music in Your Podcast

Okay, so you have an ethically and legally sourced piece of music you want to use in your show, and now you want to know the best way to effectively deploy it in your next episode. At least, I hope that's something you want to know. It's entirely possible that you took your song and then just dropped it, full blast, right on top of your show's erudite discussion about the latest episode of *Supernatural* or whatever. I'm hoping that's not the case and that the following paragraphs can help you avert that tragic fate.

First things first: your theme song.

God, please pick a good theme song.

I wrote about the friction-free nature of podcasts as a medium earlier—listeners pay nothing for your show and won't hesitate to turn it off after being exposed to an unpleasant aural experience. Your theme song is, most likely, the first thing people hear, and therefore it could easily make or break your podcast. Don't let all your recapping of the Winchester brothers' monster-hunting antics go to waste! Make your theme song something that your listeners will be excited to hear every time they hear it.

Again, musical taste is subjective, so I can talk only in general rules, using my personal preferences as a guide.

Make sure your theme song isn't, for lack of a better word,

shrill. I'm not endorsing the use of Muzak, but simply suggesting that your listeners are going to hear the song you've chosen a lot. There are certain sounds that can start to get grating when listened to ad nauseam. For example, say you want to use some chiptunes in your video game podcast. Great! Just keep in mind that a song featuring piercing, high-pitched sawtooth synths in the opening seconds of your show might prove to be too much to bear for some sensitive-eared audience members.

 To this point, use headphones when choosing music for your show. It will give you a better idea of how most folks will actually be experiencing your show.

If your theme song features vocals, make sure they don't distract from the content of your show—especially if the song underscores the show's dialogue at any point. For example, if the intro fades out as you start talking or cuts in as you go to a commercial break. Hearing one person talk while another sings can make it difficult for the brain to understand either.

 Also, be sure to look up what the lyrics actually are before you use it. You don't want to get fifty episodes in before you discover that your theme song is about kicking puppies or something.

You probably don't need me to tell you to pick a theme song that matches the vibe of your show, but darn, I've gone ahead and done it anyway. Opening up your true crime podcast with the iconic guitar riff from "Jessica" by the Allman Brothers would be . . . actually, forget what I was about to say. That would be fucking incredible. Do exactly that.

Try to pick a theme song with sections that naturally lend themselves to be your show's intro, outro, and, if necessary, interstitial music. For example, we picked "(It's a) Departure" by the Long Winters (thanks, John!) as the theme song for *My Brother, My Brother and Me*, partially because its intro is a high-energy intro for our show, its outro is a good outro for our show, and its bridge works well as our pad music as we go into commercial breaks. That might not be true of another song—maybe one with a slow and plodding intro or a meandering close.

Now, that's just advice for picking your theme song—what about a song you've chosen as background music for a segment, whether it's accompaniment to a nonfiction show or the score of a fiction podcast? What's the best way to drop that in your show? Mixing is a fine art that, to be completely frank, I do not feel nearly qualified enough to give advice on, and I have been editing podcasts professionally for ten years. Tweaking your spoken word, your background music, and whatever other tracks you've plopped onto your project timeline and *then* ensuring that their respective volumes are balanced in perfect, constant harmony—yeah, that's a tough putt.

Just starting out, though, I'd recommend erring on the side of caution. There's no rule for how much quieter your background music should be than the rest of your show. That varies quite a bit, depending on the dynamics and pitch of the song and speaker. Instead of dialing in that exact amount, just make sure that your music is turned down to the point where the spoken word content of your show is clear and understandable. Then turn the music down some more. Remember, you know what those spoken words are. You or your cohosts said them. Your brain might tell you it can hear those words over the music, when really, it's just remembering them over the music.

Securing music for your show is hard enough; don't make it something that actively detracts from the content of the show.

Another editing tip, as long as I'm harping, is to give your music nice, smooth fades and transitions whenever you incorporate it. After the main theme of our show plays, I like to give it a nice, slow fade to silence over about ten seconds or so.

When an interstitial song plays in *The Adventure Zone*, I like to slowly, quietly fade it in under the dialogue for ten seconds or so, before fading it all the way in as the segment ends. Most editing software will let you create envelopes on your tracks, allowing you to manually set their volume at specific points in the timeline. Some even include fade tools, letting you highlight a segment of audio, apply the fade, and get on with the rest of your day.

There's one last thing to talk about in this section, and I've hesitated to talk about it up until now, because it's so complicated and abstract and above my pay grade. It's time to talk about fair use.

Say you want to make a music criticism podcast where you and your cohosts play clips of new music to inspire conversation and give your audience context for your discussion. That's going to require you to include a lot of music in your show—a lot of music that, most likely, is going to require costly licenses. Can't you just . . . do it? Because of fair use?

Maybe!

There is literally no other answer to that question. Fair use isn't a hard-and-fast rule; it's a set of considerations that can help determine whether the unlicensed use of a copyrighted work is legally sound. It is open to interpretation—even if you follow its principles to the letter, it's still not an impenetrable legal bulwark against the copyright holder's interests.

If you want to include music in your show claiming fair use, there are a few things you need to ask yourself first.

> Has anyone out there ever dreamed of watching a grown man pull several paragraphs of legal-sounding text out of his ass? Keep your eyes on my brother as he does exactly that!

Are you transforming the work by including it in your show? For example, are you using it for criticism—like in the example above—news reporting, education, or research? Are you changing its purpose in the way that you use it, rather than trying to substitute its purpose? Are you using the copyrighted work in a nonprofit or noncommercial manner? Bear in mind: this is not the be-all and end-all determination. Coldplay can still come after you, even if your show isn't making any money.

How much of the copyrighted work are you including, and how important is the section you included? Here's where things get messy. Did you include too much of a song in your podcast? That is completely up to interpretation. Also, did you include the most essential part of said music? What does that even mean? Does the guitar riff from "Jessica" qualify as the "core" of that song's essence?

Now you see how fair use isn't a reliable tool for argument: it can mean anything. And, also, nothing.

 And everything. And something. And two things and new things.

Does your inclusion of the copyrighted work harm the potential value of said work? In short, will people listen to a song on your podcast and then not go buy said song from a reputable vendor, robbing the artist from a hard-earned sale? Because that would be bad, and it would also make your usage less applicable for fair use.

To summarize: claiming "fair use" when arguing the legality of your unlicensed use of copyrighted music in your podcast is tantamount to claiming that you're allowed to use Coldplay's "Viva La Vida" because Chris Martin gave you permission in a dream. It might work? If your usage of that music falls on the right side of the above criteria, you're certainly more likely to be protected—but again, it's not a sure thing.

I feel like I have to say again, here, legally, that I am not a lawyer. Nothing above is prescriptive. If this book is evidence in a court of law during a copyright infringement case, and you're a lawyer reading this out loud during my deposition or whatever: I never said I was a lawyer. They did these terrible, terrible things of their own volition and should feel just awful about it.

Whew, that was a close one.

Seeking Feedback

WITH TRAVIS MCELROY

All right, friends, we've reached a precipice. You got the equipment, you recorded a show, and you edited it. That's all the easy stuff. Now, it's time for another human being to listen to your audio baby with their human ears. Seeking feedback can be scary, but there is good news! With a few tips and tricks it can be a smooth and painless process.

Who to Ask

First, and most important, *everything is subjective*! If one of your feedbackers says that they don't like something, it can feel like you should just go ahead and cut it. But what if the thing they don't like is something you *love*? Time to take a step back and really think about it. Do you love it because you put a lot of work into it or because the finished product is good? Is the reviewer the target audience for the segment/subject in question? Is there a middle ground where you may be able to make some minor changes to end up with something you both like? In the end, it is up to you whether you keep it or kill your darling.

Travis has killed, like, a thousand podcasts he's piloted. You should pay attention, because he's definitely the authority on this.

Yeah, I just don't think we can overstate what an extensive knowledge of failure that Travis possesses. It's a miracle he's still doing this, frankly.

This is why it is important that the people who you ask for feedback are people whose opinions you trust. It can be tempting to ask your most enthusiastically supportive friend, but that might not be the feedback you need. A good rule is to seek oppo-site feedback from how you feel about the show. Think it's per-fect? Ask your most analytical friend! Think it's terrible? Ask your most supportive! The important thing is the trust factor. You might be getting *big* notes from these people and it is going to be up to you to decide whether to implement them.

Also, limit the number of people you ask for feedback. I would suggest keeping it between three and five. Too many more than that and you start to run the risk of getting a big jumble of con-flicting feedback. Additionally, it's more people to hound to get them to listen and deliver their thoughts. Start small—you can always ask more people after the first round of feedback.

When it comes to who to pick, it could be anyone! A friend, a family member, a coworker—anyone you want! I would recom-mend a few guidelines. In a perfect world, the person you pick would tick all three of the following boxes:

- You trust their opinion.
- They are a regular podcast listener.
- They have an interest in the subject matter or a related sub-ject.

It can, of course, be hard to find someone who checks off all three. In that case, I have ordered them from most important to least. As I have said, trust is very important in picking your feedbacker. Next, an understanding of the form and feel of podcasts helps inform their feedback. It can be hard for someone who has never listened to a podcast to tell you how to make yours better since they have nothing to compare it with. When it comes to interest in the subject matter, this one is least important to me. There are many shows that I appreciate even though the topic discussed is of little interest to me. I would just recommend avoiding questions about the subject unless you know that they are adept at objective judgment.

What to Ask

The time has come for me to give you the most valuable secret I have when it comes to seeking feedback. Are you ready? I can wait if you want to go get a drink first. All right, here it is. Be specific in your ask. Did you get that? I'll repeat: be specific in your ask. Just saying, "So, what did you think?" does you no good. You're likely to get something along the lines of "It was good!" Who does that help? No one, that's who. Before you give the episode to someone to listen, think about all the things about the show that you are unsure about. Then, when you give it to someone, say, "Could you do me a favor? Take a listen to this and let me know what you think about the pacing and the transitions," or whatever your concerns happen to be.

It's useful to think about feedback in terms of what human beings are hardwired to like. We don't like telling friends they made something bad. But when we get the opportunity to tweak something to make it just a little better? We love that. We could do that all day long.

Along those same lines, avoid leading and yes/no questions. They tend to stifle discussion and limit usable feedback. "Did you like the intro music?" "Yes." Does that mean they liked it for the show or that they would listen to it in their car without the show? What did they like about it? Are they just saying yes because that is what they think you want to hear? You'll get a more helpful response asking, "What did the intro music make you feel about the show?"

Other examples of what to avoid:

"Was it too long?"
"Was it boring?"
"Does the title make sense?"

Instead, try asking:

"What did you think about the length?" or "How was the pacing?"

"What are your thoughts on the subject matter?"

"What does the title tell you about the show?"

Figure out these questions ahead of time and give them to your feedbackers when you send them the episode. Guidance is *always* appreciated, and if you have avoided leading questions, they won't feel limited. Having been on the other side of this several times, let me tell you that being asked, "What did you think about the transition music?" and realizing that you didn't pay attention to the transition music isn't a great feeling.

If you have more than, say, three or four questions you want to ask, break them up among your feedbackers. You don't want to overload your friend/family member/coworker with a lengthy homework assignment. Remember, unless you have worked out some kind of trade deal or arranged to pay them in some way, they are doing you a favor.

How to Ask

This may seem obvious, but email them the audio file directly even if you asked them to listen to it face-to-face. Giving someone a bunch of search terms or a URL to remember is a good way to make sure that they never listen to the episode. You want to make it as easy as possible for them. The email is also a great way to have all your questions in one place that they can easily refer back to.

Lazy friend pro tip: Put it on YouTube and set it to unlisted, then email your friends a link. They can stream it anywhere with the click of a button.

When you ask, gently give them a deadline. Something along the lines of "I'm hoping to put this up by the end of the week, but I'd love your feedback before I do!" or "I'd love to hear your thoughts over coffee this weekend, my treat!" Listen, I know that it might seem weird to ask for a favor and in the same breath give them a time limit, but trust me when I say that they will appreciate it. If you just say, "When you get a chance!" that could mean never. Even if someone really does intend to help you out, other things can get in the way. If it doesn't seem to have any urgency, your podcast is just going to get bumped down the list. Worse, it might get completely forgotten.

By giving them a gentle deadline, you are saving yourself from having to follow up and making them feel bad for not getting to it yet. You don't want it to become a chore that carries any kind of negative connotation to it. Setting up plans to get together for coffee or lunch or even a Skype video call makes it instead feel like a fun event to look forward to!

> Provided you are a madman like my brother for whom social appointments are palatable, if not delightful. I prefer my feedback digitally transmitted to me through a cold, unfeeling screen like all other sane people.

Using the Feedback

So, you have hopefully received feedback from a couple sources . . . now what? Now you have to work on implementing said feedback. I'll refer you back to the beginning of this section and remind you that you don't have to use every piece of input gathered. That said, it is important that you carefully think through the feedback you receive. I hate to spring this on you, but you are never going to stop receiving feedback. Between reviews, social media, and people you meet in real life, you will never be able to escape the slew of thoughts and opinions about your show.

This is wonderful! It means that people care enough about

your show to form opinions! They either love it or want to help it grow! It can also help you improve as a host, a producer, and maybe even as a person! Feedback, whether positive or negative, means that people are invested! *Huzzah!*

However, it can also be a show killer. One of the biggest mistakes that people make early in their shows is to chase perfection based on audience input: "This person said they like segment A, so I'll do more of that. This person said they don't like segment B, so I'll cut it."

Listen, you can't please everyone all the time (I just made that up), and not everyone is going to love everything about your show. The key is to be open to feedback while still staying true to your vision. You need to let the feedback you receive shape the show without letting it change it into something that you no longer feel connected to. It can be an incredibly tough balance to strike, but I believe in you.

CHAPTER FIVE

Please, Someone, Anyone: Listen

Hosting

WITH JUSTIN MCELROY

Where Most Podcasts Fail

We talk to a lot of young podcasters trying to get their start, and you'd be shocked, *shocked*, by how many times we have some variation of this conversation:

"Oh, podcasting gurus, I don't know where I went wrong! I prepared for my podcast, I bought the finest microphones, and I brought on my smartest friends as cohosts. I edited and scored it to perfection and wrapped it all up with the most beautiful album art you've ever seen. But I still don't have a single listener!"

"Well, youngling," we say with gentle, wizened smiles, "what did you do with the MP3 file after you completed your first episode?"

"Well, I . . . I left it on my desktop for a while and then I deleted it the next day in frustration with my lack of response. What else would I have done with it?"

"Oh, you sweet, sweet summer child," we coo, as we scoop the amateur podcaster like a tiny infant into our burly arms, "you forgot to upload the file to a hosting service."

Don't be like this goofus. We've said it a thousand times: if you don't upload your podcast to a place where it can be downloaded by potential listeners, you're *significantly* less likely to succeed.

How Hosting Works

If you've been only a podcast consumer rather than a podcast creator to this point, there's a chance you've never interacted with a hosting service. You see, the Apple Podcasts and Pocket Casts of this world aren't where the podcasts of the world are hosted, they're more like a phone book that tells you where the podcasts live . . . What's that? What's a phone book? Well, it's sort of like a podcast directory that lists phone numbers and addresses instead of reminding you that Adam Carolla's podcast will always be more popular than yours.

A hosting service provides the house where all your beautiful little podcast files will live and be accessible to the rest of the world. They're basically just big servers to upload your data to.

Your host will create an RSS feed, which, for our purposes, can be understood as the directions to your specific house. Those directions can be fed into directories like Apple Podcasts or directly into Pocket Casts. Whenever a new episode is uploaded, the RSS feed will automatically update everyone who has subscribed to your show manually or through a service like Apple Podcasts.

Picking a Provider

We've used several different hosts over the years. We had *My Brother, My Brother and Me* on Libsyn for more than a decade, and you'll still see a lot of older podcasts using it just because it was so early in the scene. As much as we've loved dear old Libsyn, it hasn't necessarily kept up with a lot of newer services, and the interface is pretty painful. We've had shows on services like

Audioboom, Anchor, SoundCloud, ART19, and Simplecast, and they all have their strengths and weaknesses (some of which we're sure have evolved since we wrote this chapter). With so much variability, we thought we'd list some features and factors to consider when choosing podcast hosting platforms, so you can make the selection that's best for you.

One note of caution before we begin: changing hosts is a *massive* pain in the ass. Brutal, just the absolute pits. So don't rush through this part, and make sure you're settled on one before you decide to commit.

Fees: Some services offer free tiers for a small number of downloads per episode, which is a good option when you're just starting out. Remember, you can always upgrade if you outgrow a free plan. I know of at least one free plan that pulls episodes hosted with its free tier after ninety days. That seems less than great to us. Don't you want listeners to be able to enjoy the *classic* episodes that sounded like they were recorded in a trash can and featured more eating noises than a Denny's at 3:00 A.M.? Some providers will limit the number of episodes you can upload per month; some put statistics behind a paywall as well. These plans all vary wildly, so we'll just say make sure you know what you're paying for when you sign up.

Statistics: One of the most important services a host provides is data about how many times your show has been downloaded and who is listening, how they're listening, and where they're listening. A good provider will be able to show you geo-graphical data of where your show is popular (which is the number one way we decide where we'll tour *My Brother, My Brother and Me* and *The Adventure Zone*). It's also interesting to see what services people are using to listen (Spotify? Apple Podcasts? through a cup pressed against their neighbor's wall?), though this data isn't really that actionable.

Being able to chart which episodes have been downloaded the most can also help you shape the content of your show, but don't live and die by those numbers. For example, nearly every podcast we know of does worse in December. We have no idea why, but we try not to kick ourselves when it happens.

Advertising: We'll talk more about this later, but there are two important ideas we need to cover right this moment, as they relate to choosing a host: dynamic ad insertion and ad networks.

Dynamic ad insertion is basically the ability to stick ads into your show after it's been published. We're not here to tell you that dynamic advertising is right or wrong for you. But it's probably smart to choose a host with the ability to do so, should you ever decide it's something you want to pursue.

Some hosts also provide you with access to ad networks. As your show grows, many services will automatically insert ads into your show and pay a small amount for each download you receive. They may also go the old-fashioned route and provide you with ad copy to read. This can be really helpful because most sponsors won't buy space on a small show because it's not really worth their time. A hosting service can bundle several small shows together and make it worth their while.

Age and Prestige: Podcasting start-ups spring up constantly, and while they may bring glitzy features and a slick user interface, there's still the concern that they (like so many start-ups) will go belly-up and leave your show homeless. Hosts that have been around for a long time or have a major company backing them up are usually a safer bet.

Another potential indicator of a good provider is if your favorite podcasts use it (you can usually find this information on their website). Marc Maron's enormously huge *WTF* podcast uses Libsyn, Adam Carolla uses Nox, *Guys We F****d* is on Megaphone, and so on. Note that podcasts that are part of big networks will often use a large enterprise provider (like Earwolf does with Omny Studio) that may not make sense for an indie like yourself. Some other biggies host themselves, like WNYC does for *2 Dope Queens* and its other shows.

Website: Most every host will automatically generate *some* sort of web presence for your show. While it's easy enough to make your own website with a service like Squarespace or—well, there are others, but none that have been *putting food in our families' mouths for ten years*—it's nice if the starter website your host generates isn't murder on the eyes like some of the legacy providers'.

Embeddable Player: Most hosts will generate a little bit of HTML code that can be dropped onto a website and let visitors play a podcast directly from that page. Some players look really slick, some are extremely bad. Try to see a sample of what an embedded episode looks like on an external site while you're researching.

Contributions: As of this writing, this is provided only by Anchor, we believe, but we'll be surprised if others don't follow suit. On the website that Anchor generates for your show, there is a link to start a monthly contribution to your podcast—a baked-in, low-impact way to turn listeners into donors. That's cool!

Cross-Promotion: There are some providers that are just receptacles for podcasts and there are some that try to seem a little more like a cohesive network of shows. One of the ways the latter type builds a sense of community is cross-promotion, asking you to plug other shows it hosts and then other shows to do the same in return. This can be valuable for a show just getting started, so it might be a nice feature to look for.

Support: Despite our efforts to make the technical process of creating a podcast seem as easy as it (usually) is, you're bound to run into hiccups. See what the customer support for your potential provider looks like before you commit. One of the nice things about long-running providers like Libsyn is that Google is full of step-by-step troubleshooting resources and advice for navigating your hosting platform, but you can't count on that for newer services.

Take Your Time

Choosing a host is one of the few parts of the podcasting process we won't try to pretend is a breezy joy. It's a big choice, and it's one that you shouldn't rush into without doing your homework first. Choosing the wrong host, or one that can't grow alongside your show, won't make or break you. But taking the time to find the right home for your show can speed things along considerably and save you some pretty massive headaches down the road.

Climbing the Podcast Charts

WITH GRIFFIN MCELROY

So, you've got your podcast done, dusted, and uploaded to your chosen podcast host. At this point, folks with the appropriate link to your RSS feed can listen to your new show. If that's as far as you want to take this enterprise . . . I mean, that's your prerogative. I'll admit, that's got kind of a 1990s underground punk-rock VHS-trading-market vibe that I'm *super* into.

Generally speaking, though, it's good practice for people to be able to find your show without your direct intervention. Which is to say: it's time to add your show to some podcast listening platforms, such as Apple Podcasts, Spotify, Pocket Casts, or [insert relevant podcast listening platform based on the time period you're reading this book in, assuming folks are still interested in listening to podcasts in the future and aren't too busy battling each other for seeds and radiation-free water].

These platforms are often called "podcatchers." Just a cool bit of lingo for you.

There's a distinction you should understand between your podcast host and a podcast platform. When you upload an audio file to your hosting service of choice, it stores that file online and generates a link where folks can access it. It also ingests whatever data you've fed it, either per episode (the episode's title, description, album art, etc.) or per show (the show's title, your name, the content rating, etc.). A podcast platform (such as Apple Podcasts, still the most prevalent platform at the time of this writing) is where that data surfaces. Your host is where you store your finished product; Apple Podcasts and similar platforms are where it goes to market.

The good news is that getting your show on said platforms is typically quick and painless—so long as you've been thorough when setting up things on the hosting side. Most platforms simply lift all that juicy metadata from your RSS feed, rather than forcing you to fill in a lengthy application by hand for each podcast you create.

With that in mind: make sure your show's settings on your hosting platform are on point before you go any further. Is the title correct? Is the description free of glaring grammatical errors? Are you using the final album art? Are the show's category tags accurate? This information is going to be used by every platform your show ends up on, so give it a quintuple-check, just to ensure you don't spread your goof-ups far and wide.

One section of your metadata to pay special attention to is your show's **categories**. I'll explain why in a second. Now, let's get this bad boy up and into the marketplace of ideas.

Submitting Your Show to a Podcast Platform

For the purposes of our tutorial, I'm going to describe the process of getting your show on to Apple Podcasts. Bear in mind, though, that the landscape might have changed by the time you're reading this, and now Apple exclusively manufactures Faraday cages to secure your precious data cubes from the Ever-Expanding Cyberstorm.

> You'd have thought we would have seen that one becoming an issue, what with the name and all . . .

For now, it's a fitting place to start. Apple Podcasts is still where nearly half of everyone who listens to podcasts . . . listens to podcasts. Other platforms, like Spotify, are cutting into that share, but for now it's the platform supreme. Not only that, a few competing platforms—like Pocket Casts—will automatically add your show to their lineup once it appears on Apple Podcasts.

TL;DR: there's a river flowing deep and wide, and Apple Podcasts is its wellspring.

To get anything on to the Apple Podcasts ecosystem, you use a service called Podcast Connect. Go ahead and type that into your web browser and find the login splash page. Just log in using your Apple ID (which, *oh right*, you'll also need to have) and you'll end up on the Podcast Connect dashboard.

You'll want to bookmark this dashboard, because eventually, it'll give you a few pieces of *wildly* accurate analytics with regard to folks listening to your show on Apple devices. Specifically, how many devices each episode ends up on, how many hours said episode has been listened to on said devices, and what percentage of that episode's running time folks listening on said devices have finished. So, essentially, *it knows everything.*

For now, click the plus symbol, and you'll be prompted to input your show's RSS feed. Head back to your hosting service, where you should be able to easily locate said link. For Libsyn, it's right there under Destinations, labeled "Libsyn Classic Feed." *The McElroy Brothers Will Be in Trolls World Tour*'s link ends in "RSS," which is a helpful mnemonic device I use to remember which Destination is our RSS feed.

Once you've dropped that in, you'll confirm that Apple Podcasts has received all the data you've filled in with your host. It will also prompt you if there's any important data you need before you can submit your show for approval, such as categories. If you don't have any selected, Apple won't let you get past this step. Again, make sure you've selected categories that are specific and accurate before you go any further. It's kind of important.

Every time I have submitted a podcast to iTunes, I have, without fail, gotten the logo size wrong on the first try. It needs to be a minimum size of 1,400 x 1,400 pixels and a maximum size of 3,000 x 3,000 pixels.

Once everything looks good to go, click "Validate." Look out, world! Your podcast is about to hit the scene!

In one to three business days.

Damn, y'all, we should have had you do this step on page one. You're probably all horny to start your new career in podcast production, and now we've gone and slammed on the brakes. Good things come to those who wait! Assuming those who wait aren't making a podcast that includes infringing or illegal content, because Apple isn't going to let that slide.

The review process could take anywhere between a few hours to a few days, so plan your launch party accordingly. You'll receive an email confirmation once it's complete, and hopefully it will now show your podcast as "Active" on Apple Podcasts. Congratulations!

If you failed the review, it will tell you why—usually because of an error in the metadata of your RSS feed—and what steps you should take before resubmitting. Try not to take this resounding failure too hard. Pobody's nerfect!

That's just the walk-through for Apple Podcasts, but you'll find that other platforms follow similar vetting processes that you'll need to clear. For example, Spotify requires you to log in to a "Spotify for Podcasters" dashboard, where you'll plug in your RSS feed, double-check your show's metadata, then submit it for approval.

If you're trying to get in front of as many folks as possible from the jump, you may as well sow your oats by looking up the most popular platforms at the moment (Apple Podcasts, Spotify, Stitcher, etc.) and getting your show on them.

Climbing the Charts

There are a few different vectors through which your podcast can achieve success, and, to be perfectly frank, podcast platform discoverability isn't the most effective among them. We'll have more on how to promote your show a bit later on, and that's going to be the process through which you'll get most of your new listeners—not because your show landed at #26 on the earth sciences charts.

Still, *can't hurt*, right?

 Way down the line, being able to say, "The show hit number blah on the such-and-such charts," can be useful if you are trying to court advertisers or pitch your show to be hosted on a podcast network.

Continuing to use Apple Podcasts as the template, there are a few things to keep in mind if you want listeners to organically find your show on-platform. The most important factor to keep in mind is—thanks for waiting for this explanation, by the way—the categories you've selected for your show.

At the time of writing, Apple Podcasts lists podcasts under nineteen top-level categories, most of which further break down into more granular, more specific subcategories. You want your show to appear in its relevant category, mostly because it inherently makes it more visible on the platform, but also because each subcategory has its own chart. The more specific the category, the less competition you've got, and the more likely it is that your show will chart.

It's worth noting that the "chart" I'm describing isn't strictly a measurement of who's got the most listeners. The exact math that goes into Apple Podcasts rankings is shrouded in mystery, but anecdotally speaking, these charts value newness and growth as much as they value total audience size. (This is good news for you, the creator of a *new* podcast.)

Garnering even a modest number of listeners during your first couple of weeks will *dramatically* increase your chances of hitting one of the Apple Podcasts charts. In fact, you might hit multiple: if your show falls under a subcategory, it's considered for the charts of that subcategory, the top-level category, and the default "All Podcasts" ranking.

Once the shine's come off the Apple (lol), you'll have to work *way* harder to keep or boost your spot in the rankings. You stand a chance if you maintain a steady increase of listeners as you continue, but in general, it takes an act of God to change up the top ten shows in a major category. (*My Brother, My Brother and Me* is #19 on the comedy charts at the moment, where it usually lingers, well behind Joe fucking Rogan and his apparently impregnable podcast battleship.)

And if you don't make it? Seriously, don't sweat it. Not that many folks are going to stumble upon their new favorite show while browsing the rankings of an Apple Podcasts subcategory. If anything, folks are going to stumble upon their new favorite show—ideally *your show*—by searching for it on-platform. That search scans the title and description of not just your show but every episode you've ever published.

To summarize, rather than trying to game the system, it's way more important for you to include thorough descriptions and SEO-friendly titles when publishing new episodes. It makes it way more likely that folks will find your show when searching for a certain topic, which is always going to be a more effective lure than "Hey, give my podcast a spin, it's only thirty-seven podcasts less popular than Joe fucking Rogan's."

Communicating with Listeners

WITH JUSTIN MCELROY

I'm sorry that it has taken this long to tell you, truly, but there is no surefire way to succeed in podcasting. Or anything really. But definitely podcasting. That being said, there is one thing that we feel fairly sure that, without it, you stand no chance of building a sustainable audience.

If we have a secret sauce, a magic trick, that has helped us become a success despite our mediocrity in many areas you would think important for professional talkers (bad recording equipment, bad voices, etc.), then it would be this: we actually, no bullshit, appreciate our listeners.

We don't want to pat ourselves on the backs too much for this—it's a pretty low bar to clear as a human being. Again, if someone is nice enough to give you their most precious resource (their life minutes), then we believe you owe it to them to not make them feel like they've wasted their time. You do that in lots of ways that we've talked about already or will soon. You care about the quality of your sound, you edit out the boring stuff, and you create a recording plan so you make the best end product you can.

In this section, we'll be talking about something a little more direct: communicating with listeners to make sure they understand that if they're listening to you, you're also listening to them.

I can actually track the development of this radical policy of giving a crap about people to the Dale Carnegie audiobooks I listened to on cassette when I was an unpopular teenager desperate to win friends and/or influence people. He tells the story of meeting magician Howard Thurston (he was a big deal back in the day) and asking him the secret of his success. I've copied his answer here verbatim.

> HE TOLD ME that many magicians would look at the audience and say to themselves, "Well, there is a bunch of suckers out there, a bunch of hicks: I'll fool them all right." But Thurston's method was totally different. He told me that every time he went on stage he said to himself: "I am grateful because these people come to see me. They make it possible for me to make my living in a very agreeable way. I'm going to give them the very best I possibly can."
>
> He declared he never stepped in front of the foot-

lights without first saying to himself over and over: "I love my audience. I love my audience." Ridiculous? Absurd? You are privileged to think anything you like. I am merely passing it on to you without comment as a recipe used by one of the most famous magicians of all time.

If you want our secret to success, here it is: we love our audience. This section is about how you can let them know.

The Old-Fashioned Email

Communication is vital to your growing podcast, but you can't expect your early listeners to open those lines of communication up. That's your job, unfortunately.

The first, most obvious, and most direct way to encourage listeners to reach out is by creating a simple email address that you include in every episode. Gmail is fine, but if you can't find a succinct email address, it may be worth spending $12 so you can register a domain and get a really short one. It also just sounds a bit more professional.

Social media is great, and we'll discuss that soon, but you can't beat email for more in-depth (and private) communication. If you're just getting started, it's worth responding to as much email as you comfortably can.

Let's say you start with a single listener. That one person represents the only chance you have at building an audience. They are your only hope, the bearer of the tiny flicker of popularity your show has, and you want them to go into the world and spread the word. You can't pay this single candle bearer to go out there and set the world ablaze for you—all you can do is let them know how meaningful their time is to you and how much you appreciate them passing the show along to others.

It may seem like we're being dramatic, but it's tough to overstate how fragile your audience is at this point and how much impact you can have by treating each listener like a valuable human being who holds your future in their hands (which they are).

Thank You for Not Sharing

Besides being a great way to stay in touch, emails can also provide content for your show. *My Brother, My Brother and Me* is an advice show and obviously lives and dies by questions that our listeners send our way, to say nothing of the weird internet ephemera they dig up and pass along.

Emails can make for great discussion starters; even just introducing a new voice via email can provide a shot in the arm. It's like bringing on a guest you can kick off whenever you like and give a hard time without them being able to contradict all your great jokes.

Reading email is also a great way to encourage getting more email, as everyone loves the idea that they'll be featured in a show that they enjoy.

Wait, did that paragraph say *"everyone loves the idea"*? I'm so sorry, I don't know why it says that. That paragraph has been slacking off a lot lately—troubles at home maybe? Who knows. Anyway, not *everyone* loves the idea of having their email read aloud.

If you want to read an email on the show, you need to be absolutely confident that the sender intended it for mass consumption. If someone sends a request for advice into *My Brother, My Brother and Me*, we feel pretty confident including it, even without their explicit permission. But if there's a stitch of doubt in our mind, we confirm that it's okay to read.

If your show doesn't typically make listener emails a part of it, you need to make doubly sure that the sender of an email wants it blasted out to the wider world. There's no taking that back.

How to Love a Troll

We've talked about the importance of communication, but not necessarily the content of those communications and how to handle them. Put simply: If the email is positive, be effusive in your gratitude. If it's constructively critical, be even more appreciative. If it's mean and shitty . . . well, then it gets less simple.

There is absolutely nothing wrong with deciding you don't have it in you to fuck around with someone who's acting like a total creepazoid. And if they're clearly trolling you, that's probably the right call. But if you can find it in your heart to tell that person you're sorry that you wasted their time, that you hope they find another podcast they enjoy more, and that you appreciate them giving you a shot? You'll be shocked, *shocked*, at how often you can create a lifelong fan.

It always amazes me how often people who send mean messages, when responded to, will say, "Oh! I didn't think you'd ever see this!" Not everyone grew up with instant messengers and chat rooms. A lot of folks see the internet as a void to be screamed into and don't always imagine someone listening. This is not to excuse shitty behavior in the least. Just a reminder that not everything is a personal attack! I am reminded of a time when someone was tweeting about how much they hated being at one of our live shows. I contacted them and they turned out to be a very nice person who was just going through a really rough time. That said, I also know that my day-to-day load of emotional labor is pretty light. It's not your job to turn every negative reviewer into a fan—we're just saying that it can be done!

The internet breeds apathy. You have no way of knowing how many times the person on the other line has been ignored and treated like nothing. By treating someone with basic decency, you may do something much more important than create a fan; you could remind that hard-hearted person that there are still people out there who give a shit.

Or maybe just delete it, that's fine too. Life is short. It's your call.

Email Is for Old People

One other note about email is that nobody writes emails anymore. Well, maybe old people do, but not young folks like all of us in our physical and sexual prime. What use do we have for emails? We've got social media.

We're not going to talk about marketing your show via

social media here (that's a whole other chapter to look forward to). In fact, we'd like to stick with Twitter for the moment, as we've found Facebook to be a less-effective place for one-on-one communication with listeners.

The most important thing to remember when interacting with listeners on Twitter is that everyone is watching. Well, they're not, but they could be, and that should make you think super extra hard about how you present yourself when communicating with a listener. It's not like you're a secret creep in one-on-one emails (those emails can still be screenshotted, and besides, you're already a nice person, right?). But on Twitter, the public nature creates additional risks:

1. Every comment can be taken out of context and retweeted to a giant audience.
2. Followers often take tweets as an opportunity to comment or spin off their own discussions.

This makes Twitter a bad environment for meaningful discussion. No, scratch that, it's a 100 percent terrible environment for meaningful discussion forever and ever, always.

The watchwords then are "brevity," "positivity," and "gratitude." The key thing to do is acknowledge that you've seen the tweet and then thank them for it in the most positive way you can muster. You do not, *must not*, get into an argument on Twitter. No one will win. Please, you don't have to do it. Don't do it. It will end badly.

We mentioned in the last segment about winning over detractors over email, but this is riskier on social media. What can feel meaningful to a critic in private can seem performative in public. If you see a baseless or cruel tweet about your show, you're almost always best served by muting the person and moving on.

Gather in Our Name

We've tried some nontraditional methods of connecting with our listeners over the years, some of which haven't been a good fit and others that gave us a great boost in the early days.

We know some shows use them to great effect, but opening up a voicemail line was a time sink for us and attracted a lot of . . . odd contributions. More frustratingly, it's not like we were going to call anyone back, so it felt like a very one-dimensional tool for building relationships. Still, we know some shows swear by them (*Uhh Yeah Dude* has kept its open for more than a decade, so what do we know?).

Our little gimmick (to which we've often attributed a lot of our early growth) was listening parties. The idea was this: whenever a listener could get four or more people together to listen to an episode of *My Brother, My Brother and Me*, we would record a personal greeting to play before their party. They would send us the names of attendees beforehand, and all they had to do in exchange was send us photo proof of the party.

This worked beautifully, especially for a podcast just finding its legs. Recording the messages was easy, and we met a lot of lovely listeners we're still in contact with today this way. Eventually we had to ease off the listening parties, as the show grew to a point where we would have been spending all our days recording greetings. Still, if you're just starting out, it's a fun idea.

A Face for Radio

If you're at this long enough, you're eventually going to meet listeners in person. Depending on your temperament, this is either extremely exciting to look forward to or genuinely terrifying. We can work with either impulse.

(Personal interaction is, admittedly, a little ways down the road if you're just starting out. Maybe come back when you're ready, or just keep reading. What do we care, it's your book!)

If the idea of face-to-face hangs isn't too much for you, you could always orchestrate one yourself by organizing a meetup.

It's easy enough to announce you'll be at a bar or at Dave & Buster's and just hope people show up. If you're comfortable with it, it's hard to beat that level of intimacy for building an audience.

For my money, you can't go wrong with a bar with board games. Something for folks to do and socialize, while also giving you room to move around and schmooze!

Keep in mind, though, that even if you have a decent audience, they're probably spread out across the country (and world), so you may not be able to draw a crowd in your hometown. That's okay! Don't get frustrated. Just try to have a good rapport with the few that do show, or, you know, enjoy a relaxing drink on your own.

You can work around this by planning meetups while visiting big conventions!

Even if you don't seek it out, meeting listeners may one day be foisted upon you, be it after a live recording or by the random hand of fate. Here's our very quick guide to handling these interactions well:

1. Warmly greet the person, say it's a pleasure to meet them (it is, remember), make sure to get their name.

2. If they seem really nervous, you'll probably have to control the interaction. Don't wait for them to lead the conversation; this is bound to be a little weird for them.

3. If you don't feel silly about it, you can offer to take a picture, or maybe they've already asked. Either way, great! But . . .

4. Before you throw your arm around someone for a photo, make sure they're cool with it. It's awkward to ask, "Is it okay if I touch you?" but not as awkward as touching someone who'd really rather you not.

5. If the listener is especially uncomfortable, they may not know how to end the conversation. That's fine, you just need to take control again and end the interaction just the way you began it, with warmth and gratitude.

I Love My Audience

We've thrown out a lot of dictates and guidelines here, but they can all be summarized in a single concept that we introduced at the beginning of the section: respect. We've never thought of our audience as a series of earholes. We've tried to think of them as people, because that's how they think of themselves, and, frankly, it's the only moral thing to do.

Show respect for the time the listener has spent on your show, respect for their support, and gratitude for the energy they've infused into your creation with their mere attention, and you're going to create an audience that can feel good about listening to what you make and sharing it with friends.

Our one-on-one marketing strategy isn't any more complicated than this: treat people like people.

The Obligatory Social Media Chapter

WITH TRAVIS MCELROY

Well, my friends, the time has come. You see, you're attempting to get a product in front of a consumer, and it's after 2004. That means it's time for the obligatory social media chapter!

Wait! Don't go! I promise this isn't going to be about "going viral" and memes and stuff. (But give memes a chance, a lot of them are kinda funny.)

 My brother sounds like he's a sixty-five-year-old cop trying to sneak his way into the Cool Teen Internet Zone. Please do not stop reading this book because of this.

We're going to teach you about *practical*, real-world ways to use social media to grow your show and, hopefully, your audience.

So, in the before time/the long, long ago, social interaction on the internet mostly took place in chat rooms. For anyone reading this who was born after the year 2000, imagine the early internet as a long hallway lined with doors all labeled with *very* specific interests. You'd find a room where people were discussing what you wanted to talk about and you'd go in. The problem with this structure, at least as far as we are concerned, was that you could only reach the people already in that room and the rooms were quite small. If you found yourself in a room with more than one hundred people, it was a rare experience.

Then came Facebook (after Myspace and Friendster, R.I.P.) and that changed. This new site allowed you to post things and discuss them publicly. It opened up conversations—for better or worse—to a much wider audience. However, that audience was still limited to people you were connected to.

It is no coincidence that the boom of podcasting and the

advent of the Twitter age go hand in hand. With Twitter, there was the chance that *anyone* might find your show or website or blog or whatever! Complete strangers might stumble across a link and become fans.

Now listen, far smarter folks than us will spend the next twenty years or more debating whether the existence of social media is a societal net positive.

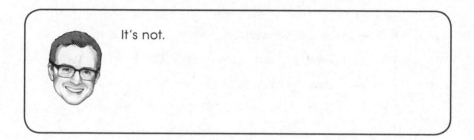

It's not.

But we are not interested in that at the moment. We are looking at it purely as a means to an end.

The first thing you need to keep in mind is that "social media" is a blanket term for a *huge* collection of things. Oftentimes, people tend to think only of Facebook or Twitter, but there's also [big breath in] Instagram, Snapchat, Tumblr, Reddit, Pinterest, TikTok, YouTube, Discord, Mastodon, Twitch, and many more. Not only that, there seem to be new ones being developed all the time!

Do you need to be active on all these platforms to be

successful? Nope! In fact, if you tried that, you'd spend more time on social media than you would on your podcast. We just want to make sure that you are aware of all your options so you can figure out which one works best for your show.

Which brings us to the second important thing to learn about social media. You need to separate your social media presence from the show's. Believe it or not, most of your audience is going to want show updates without also being subjected to your hot takes on movies and politics. So, as soon as your show has a name, you're gonna start registering for social media accounts (and an email address, remember?). The bad news is every single combination of words is already taken, so you'll need to get creative. Keep in mind that people will be hearing you say it instead of reading it, so make sure it is easy to spell and is spelled like it sounds. If possible, try to keep the username consistent across as many social media platforms as you can so it is easier to find.

> We didn't do a great job of this when we launched *The Adventure Zone*. For reasons that have been lost to time immemorial, we went with @TheZone Cast on Twitter, which isn't the name of our show, isn't an abbreviation we've ever used, and also sounds like a podcast about the Zone Diet, which

> we aren't even familiar with enough to make a joke here about. Don't be like us!

You've got all your various accounts registered; now it's time to get yourself some art! Let's assume by this point that you have a logo for your show, and that's great! What's that? We haven't told you to get some art? Uhhhh . . .

Welcome to a Section within a Section!

Get Some Art!

First and foremost, have someone who knows what they are doing make your art. That might be you or it might be someone you hire, but this is going to be the image associated with your show, so it needs to look good. Notice I said "hire" there. That is because if you get someone else to design your logo, you are going to pay them. This is for two very important reasons. First, you should pay people for their work, plain and simple. Second, you want to make sure you own this art because you will be using it professionally. If you are on a budget (and who isn't, amirite?!), be sure to tell the person what you are able to pay them before you commission them to do the work. It is quite possible that the amount you can afford won't cover their quote, and it's best to find that out up front. In the past, I have paid anywhere from $100 to $500 for album art, depending on how complicated the project is.

When it comes to finding someone to do your design, assuming you don't already have someone in mind, start by looking at fan art for something you like. Search through Tumblr and Twitter and whatever until you find an artist whose style you like and reach out to them. Another option is to reach out to friends who have commissioned designs or reach out to other podcasts whose logos you like and ask who did theirs.

We're no lawyers, but we'd recommend getting something on paper or in an email agreement about who owns the art and how it will be used. We've never done formal signed contracts or anything, but if you wanna be extra careful, go nuts.

When it comes to the logo itself, that's where it starts to get subjective. We can't tell you exactly what the logo should look like because it needs to match you and your show. Some things we can say are:

- It needs to be square. Podcatchers use square logos. Even if your design isn't a square itself, it needs to look good in a square frame.
- If the title is the featured element in the design, it should be prominent and easy to read.
- The logo needs to be distinct. It doesn't have to be entirely unique and break every mold, but it shouldn't be easily confused for another show's logo.
- A lot of the time, the logo is only going to be seen as a tiny thumbnail. Make sure it still works if it is shrunk down.
- Pay attention to size requirements of podcatchers. For example, Apple Podcasts requires that the image be between 1,400 x 1,400 and 3,000 x 3,000 pixels.

One other good idea is to look at other podcasts in your genre and see what kind of art they use and let that be your jumping-off point. In some genres (especially celebrity-centric shows) photography is really common. Not saying you have to ape those who have come before—maybe standing out is a smart strategy—but it doesn't hurt seeing what other successful shows are doing.

Past that, it's up to you! One subjective piece of advice that I (Travis) will give you: I think that someone should be able to look at your logo and get a general sense of what your podcast is. Even if the actual subject matter isn't represented, people should be able to get a feel for it as lighthearted or educational or narrative or what have you.

Wow, that sure is some beautiful podcast art you have there! Unfortunately, it's probably not going to work for your social media needs. For an example of what I mean, you needn't look any further than the difference between a Twitter profile picture and Twitter banner art. The size specifications are wildly different, and this is the same platform we're talkin' about! Once you get into the specifications across all platforms, it can start to feel overwhelming. Worry not, we have two solutions and you should use both. First, have in mind which platforms you are aiming for when you have the logo designed. Make sure the designer has the specifications for each platform you are planning to use and have that included as part of the design. It should go without saying, but be sure to compensate them for this extra work. Second, have your designer create individual pieces of the design that you can mix and match later to meet any requirements you need. For example, have them give you a chunk of the background layer with nothing on it, the text of the logo with no background, and maybe a recognizable piece of the image to use as flair.

Okay, got your art needs all sorted? Great! Now, back to . . .

Social Media (cont.)

Now you need to decide what you are going to post on your show's social media page. The obvious answer is that you're going to post every time an episode goes up, and you should! That said, you're going to need to do more than that. You need to give your audience some fun stuff, too. Do polls about issues you discussed on the show, share fan art, link articles related to the show's subject matter, share behind-the-scenes pictures, and/ or anything else engaging you can think of. Make your show's online presence something that your audience is excited to be a part of and to share.

One of the things that makes podcasts so special is the high level of interactivity they offer the audience. I like to think of this as a tradition passed down from radio. Much like how people used to call in with requests and long-distance dedications, folks can now tweet questions and email topic suggestions. Make sure that you plan for this!

Now, when an episode does come out or you have an important announcement, you *should* tweet about it, and you should tweet more than you probably feel like you should! The half-life of a tweet is twenty-four minutes, according to Hootsuite. That means that 50 percent of a tweet's engagement happens in the twenty-four minutes after you hit Tweet. So, you can't just say Episode is up! at 9:00 A.M. and expect people to still be seeing it in the afternoon. Now listen, I know you are going to feel like you are annoying everyone when you tweet about your show three to five times in one day, but you are looking at it all wrong. You are not standing in front of your followers yelling at them with a megaphone. You are pinning your flyer to a big bulletin board that is constantly filling up. You have to keep posting new flyers or your message will get buried!

Now that you're generating content on your various social media platforms, you're going to need to convince people to look at it. Welcome to the unending cycle of using your podcast to tell people to follow you on social media so you can then use your social media to make sure people listen to your podcast. I know that on the surface this seems unnecessary, but, in reality, it is of the utmost importance. You have to remember that we live in a world full of distractions looking to engage your audience. You're competing not only with other podcasts but with all media. Social media posts function as routine little reminders that your show exists. That's not the only reason to keep up with your social media! There's also the hope that people will share posts of yours or discuss you in posts of their own, thus getting more people interested.

Now when I listed a bunch of social media sites, did I say YouTube? Indeed I did, reader! You may not think of YouTube as a social media platform, but I promise you that YouTube is a thriving community all its own. We spent many years undervaluing having a strong presence on YouTube and we regretted it! If you want to really use the platform to its fullest, shareable clips is the way to go. Creating short clips (five minutes or less) that showcase your show, or even unique video content specifically for YouTube, gives your audience even more ways to share your content and convert new listeners/viewers!

A section on social media would not be complete if we didn't talk about Facebook. Keep in mind that we are all old, but there was a time when you weren't a thing if you didn't have a Facebook fan page/group. See, there used to be these things that were kind of like chat rooms called "forums."

 Elderly Cop Travis is back, and he's trying to sell you some bootleg vape pens. Don't fall for it! That's entrapment!

People would go to these forums to start/contribute to discussions regarding things they cared about. You're probably thinking, "Hey, that sounds like Reddit!" and you would be right, but Reddit has not always been as mainstream as it is now. When the old forums died away, people turned to Facebook groups to have these discussions. That included us.

Let me tell you what I wish I had known then: you do not need to start/run your own Facebook group. In fact, I'll extend that beyond Facebook to say that you should not create/run any kind of discussion group about your show whatsoever.

First, it's a ton of work. You'll need to manage member requests, approve posts, settle disputes, and much more. It can end up being a job in and of itself. Think of it this way: Do you think Ted Danson has time to run a forum for *The Good Place*?

Even if Ted Danson *did* have time to run that forum, he still shouldn't because of power dynamics! Say someone puts up a post about *The Good Place* in which they express their distaste for Ted's performance in a certain episode. If Ted were to respond to this, calling this person out, can you imagine how poorly that would go?! You might be thinking, "But I'm not Ted Danson. I'm just someone with a handful of listeners!" Yes, but to that handful of listeners, you are the creator of a show they love! You have way more power in this situation than they do, and it isn't fair to anyone to have you running the forum.

The final (and most important) reason not to start your own discussion group is: you don't need to. We're talking about the internet here, folks. If people want to discuss something, they will. They don't need you to create a space for them to do it.

Now, if you still want a presence on Facebook, you can always create a fan page. A fan page can act as a pseudo-website for you to post updates and pertinent information about the show without the need for full-time moderation. That said, if it becomes worth the time, effort, and hosting costs, an actual website would serve almost the exact same purpose and give you way more customizability.

Finally, I want to share some important lessons I have learned about *how* to process social media feedback. First, learn to tell the difference between constructive criticism and personal preference. I try to read between the lines to see if the comment boils down to either "it would be better if" or "I would like it better if."

Second—and this was a hard-learned lesson for yours truly—don't seek out negativity. If you are like me, when you see a bunch of people respond positively, there is something in your brain that feels the need to dig deeper and find someone who hates your pod. Try to kick that habit as soon as you can!

Third, if someone is upset about or hurt by something you said or did, don't dismiss it. It's easy to get defensive, but everyone's experience and perspective are different. Not only will you expand your own understanding of the world by learning from others, but also you may find that the quality of your show improves as well!

CHAPTER SIX
Making Money

Selling Merch

WITH JUSTIN MCELROY

Finally, we can get to the real reason anybody starts a podcast.

Or does anything, really.

You've waded through the muck and mire of coming up with an original idea and buying microphones and even uploading your show to the internet, but now, finally, the finish line is in sight.

It's finally time for you to sell some fucking T-shirts.

You've probably already found yourself perusing NonDis countedYachts.com, and I get it, I do, but you've got to restrain yourself for a few weeks until the money starts pouring in. If you go in without a plan, you're not going to become as rich as you possibly could, and you could end up buying a sixty-foot-yacht when you could have afforded a seventy-footer, and what could be sadder than that?

Let's Get Rich (Eventually)

There's a pretty easy way to know if you're ready to start producing merchandise for your show: Has anybody, I mean *anybody*, actually asked for it? If not, maybe it's worth holding off and focusing on building your show's audience.

It's not as though you're leaving piles of money on the table by holding off until you're really ready to open up a storefront. In fact, you might just be saving yourself a ton of headache by waiting for the right time.

When we started *My Brother, My Brother and Me*, we rushed to start selling T-shirts and mugs with the first independent merch partner who came calling. We were lucky that he ended up doing a good job and didn't, you know, rob us blind, steal all our designs, and sell our credit card info to Russian hackers. Again, we were lucky.

But soon, as our audience grew, we outgrew our original partner and had to completely reinvent our strategy for merchandising the show. We have now done this *multiple times*, and it has yet to get less annoying or time consuming.

If you wait until your audience is more consistent before you consider merch, then you're going to save yourself a couple of reinventions. Also, frankly, it can look a little crass for a brand-new show with no audience to come out of the gate with something to sell. Focus on audience building until the demand for merch exists.

Why Do We Merch?

Merchandise seems like a given for any cultural enterprise at this point, but before you jump in, I think it's worth considering why you're making it.

I have heard a lot of people (myself included) espouse its value as a marketing tool, but I'm somewhat suspicious of its usefulness at this point. I did an informal Twitter poll, and of the 6,500 respondents, only 12 percent said that they had ever, even one time, listened to a podcast because they saw its name on a T-shirt. Many of those in that narrow minority said that it was usually just the tipping point for checking out a show. They had heard friends talk it up, they had heard it plugged elsewhere, whatever, and the shirt was just what put them over the edge.

Maybe you're doing it for profit, but, joking aside, you're (probably) going to be looking at pretty narrow margins on the stuff you sell. Unless you garner a significant audience, you'll be lucky to afford a thirty-foot yacht and you're basically just talking about a cabin cruiser and *what's even the point?*

I would argue that the best reason to create merch is to continue to foster a connection between you and your audience. I'm not wearing my *Ear Hustle* shirt at this exact moment to win over new converts (that would be insane, I don't leave the house). I'm wearing it because it's a show I love, and it makes me feel good to wear it, to be a little bit connected to that show as I go about my day. Also, it is soft.

When I wear podcast shirts in public, I rarely find myself pitching a new show to the uninitiated. More commonly, I find that they help me start conversations with existing listeners of the show and make a connection that didn't already exist.

If you see merch as part of a broader conversation between you and your listeners (and maybe a way to cover your hosting costs), you're going to fare a lot better.

Okay, Now We Can Get Rich

There are three basic options to consider when you're going to create merch for your show.

1. Do it yourself
2. Let someone else do it
3. Something in between

Let's talk pros and cons for each approach. We'll mostly be talking about T-shirts in this section, but this is pretty much applicable to all merch.

Do It Yourself: This would entail finding a printer in your area who can create shirts for you, paying for a bunch of shirts to be printed, setting up an online storefront using a service like Shopify or Squarespace, and then shipping those orders out yourself as they come in.

This is, by a country mile, the most profitable way of merchandising. It's also vastly more time consuming than other methods. I got annoyed just writing that paragraph, and I didn't have to get out of my chair. It's also—if you're anything like me—the method with the highest likelihood of orders getting completely screwed up, and then you've alienated a listener and created the exact opposite of your intended result.

Did I mention it's the riskiest? You'll have to guess at overall demand, then specific demand for different sizing options, and *then* you'll have to pay for all of it up front. Guess wrong and you'll pay for shirts you don't need or run out of shirts that people want.

I know shows that've done it all on their own and I respect them. I just absolutely can't fathom it.

Let Someone Else Do It: You already feel better, don't you? Is there any finer feeling than completely passing off responsibility and forgetting it ever existed? I'd wager there is not.

With this approach, you'll upload a design (let's start with your show logo) to a service like TeeSpring, Society6, or Zazzle and let listeners order directly from there. The service will print your design on a wide variety of products in a rainbow of colors all on demand. Listeners will get exactly the product they want, and all you have to do is collect the checks.

This is obviously infinitely less hassle than the first method, but it's also a lot less profitable. If you're less concerned about making money (and that's probably sane early on), this would be a great way to start.

Something in Between: At this point, this is where the McElroy family of podcasts finds itself. We have a partnership with a company called DFTBA, and it handles all our printing and fulfillment. We also have a very talented and smart merchandise director who creates a lot of our designs and helps us decide what items would do well.

Another hybrid approach would be doing your printing through an on-demand service like Printful and then selling merch through your own storefront. This method would give you more control and maybe a slightly higher profit than an all-in-one solution, but it would create a little more hassle.

Personally, I doubt most shows need this level of fine control over their merchandise, especially in the early days. My advice: start with an all-in-one service and hope that you outgrow it.

> Remember that unless you're creating your own designs, you need to pay someone to make them for you. After plenty of trial and error, we tend to prefer offering a flat licensing fee for the initial design and then a royalty from our partner DFTBA on each item sold. This guarantees that the designer will be paid for their work, with the bonus that they'll make more if people really love it.

The World Beyond Shirts

We've been using T-shirts interchangeably with merchandise up to this point, and there's good reason for it. Shirts are sort of a default mode for a lot of podcasters getting into merchandise. They're reasonably priced, allow fans to recognize each other in public, and provide limited protection to the human body from the ravages of nature. Hooray for shirts!

Stickers are also cheap to make and easy to ship, which can

make them an appealing early offering. They're also great give-aways at live events if you end up with more than you can sell.

We've also done really well with enamel pins, even going so far as to have a pin-of-the-month design, which allows us to deploy and sunset new designs regularly. Our success with pins may have to do with the fact that our audience is very fun and cool. If you are targeting an audience that is more boring or full of olds (a show about taxes, for example), you may want to consider, like . . . ballpoint pens?

Pins are interesting, because they've become a big part of the zeitgeist only in the past couple of years. (That may be because they cost around $2.50 to produce and sell for $10 and up.) Maybe they're a trend that will have died out by the time you read this, which is a good reminder to look around and see what others are having success with before you launch a new product.

Very broadly speaking, we have found less success with items that won't be seen in public—postcards and home decor and the like. We still experiment with them, though, especially for items that we think are funny.

We once offered a very folksy cross-stitched wall hanging that read IN THIS HOUSE WE DON'T SAY "HAPPY HOLIDAYS" WE SAY "PODCASTS." It didn't move a lot of units, but the people who it connected with seemed to really get a kick out of making it part of their holiday decor.

Quoth the Podcast, "Here's a Shirt"

So, you started with slapping your logo on shirts: that was smart. But now that you're a little more established, you may want to get a little bit more esoteric.

Pretty much all of our designs at this point are references to characters or quotes from one of our shows. If listeners seem to really connect with certain parts of your show—favorite jokes, etc.—that may be a good place to start looking for new designs.

While it's cool if someone has heard of the podcast advertised on your shirt, getting a compliment about a specific gag that you're referencing can feel like a secret language among fellow fans. It's powerful stuff. We've gone too esoteric, for sure, so try to listen to your gut.

Generally speaking, I prefer designs that connect even if you've never heard of a show. *My Favorite Murder*'s tagline is "Stay Sexy and Don't Get Murdered," which makes for a funny T-shirt even if you've never heard of the show. We've done pro-vaccine pins for *Sawbones* that connect with both listeners and those who care about public health. (We donate the profits from those items, which . . . well, I can't say it's a good business strategy, but it feels good, and what the hell else are we doing here on this planet?)

Wait, What Do You Mean You're Not Rich?

Sorry we didn't manage to deliver on our promises of life-changing wealth, we got a little carried away in the beginning.

You can't blame us for getting excited about merchandise, though. It's a great way to connect with fans and, more important, help them connect with each other. Plus, one time a guy wore a *My Brother, My Brother and Me* shirt on *Tosh.0*, so, you know, there's that to consider.

That said, we'll close this section with a solemn promise. If we ever *do* figure out the secret for getting fabulously wealthy with podcast merchandise, we will share it with you.

In the next edition of this book.

Available in fine bookstores everywhere.

Crowdfunding

WITH TRAVIS MCELROY

Hey, money is pretty cool, right? I've heard—and don't quote me on this—that it makes the world go 'round! Well, I have some bad news for you, friend: it's hard to make money as an entertainer, and that includes podcasting. In fact, it *especially* applies to podcasting, because as a newer media it can be hard to convince bigwigs holding bags with dollar signs on them to hand you said moneybags.

So, here's an idea I just came up with: ignore the bigwigs and get funded by a crowd! I call it "crowdfunding," and it's going to change your life!

I (Travis) am of the opinion that crowdfunding is, in almost every way, the superior monetization option for podcasts. Where most options reward audience *size*, crowdfunding rewards audience *dedication*, and I think the latter is far more valuable.

Look at it this way: say you have an audience of five hundred dedicated listeners who never miss an episode. Sadly, that's not a number that would make advertising partners salivate. However, if each one of them gave you $5 a month, you're making $30k a year off your show!

Now, before you start your crowdfunding campaign, there are some options, factors, and best practices you need to know. First, let's go over your structure options.

Lump Sum

If you're thinking about sites like Kickstarter, Indiegogo, Go-FundMe, or anything that shares their model, you're talking about lump sum crowdfunding. Your fund-raising campaign will have a beginning and an end. When it finishes you will (hopefully) get a lump sum payment to help you fund your show. Within the lump sum model, there are also different options. For example, Kickstarter campaigns are all or nothing, which means if you don't hit your goal, you don't get any funds. Indie-gogo and GoFundMe give you the option of collecting whatever is pledged when the campaign ends whether you've hit your goal or not.

"Wait!" I hear you say (because I am always listening). "If that's the case, why would I not choose to have the option of collecting funds no matter what? Seems like the obvious choice!"

Well, not necessarily. Let's say you have sat down and figured out that, for example, you can't afford to buy the equipment you need, hire voice actors, and pay an editor unless you raise $1,500. At the end of your campaign, you have only raised $750. Now you have both not enough money *and* a bunch of backers who still expect to get what they paid for. If instead you just need *some* money in order to facilitate working on the project, you might opt for the take-what-you-can-get option.

The other benefit to all or nothing is psychological. Ask anyone who has run a Kickstarter campaign, and they will tell you the same thing: there is a bump as time runs out. If someone is considering donating, seeing that they could be the one who gets you over the finish line might be the motivation they are waiting for.

There are a couple of pros and cons to the lump sum model.

Pros: A big influx of funds right at the beginning, and you know you have the money you'll need to make it work. Also, the campaign itself can serve to get folks excited for your show. Cons: It can be hard to budget in advance for unforeseen expenses. Plus, if after the show has launched, you experience significant audience growth, you will need to wait to run another campaign and receive that financial benefit. And every year/season, you will need to run the campaign again.

Incremental

If you're considering a Patreon, or a patron-based, model, then you are considering incremental funding. You will get a payment every month, every time an episode goes up, or whatever the increment ends up being. Over the last few years, this model has become more and more popular. Nowadays, it's rare to find an online creator who doesn't rely on patrons for funding.

Your patrons will commit to some level of recurring financial support. As I mentioned, this is usually monthly. However, there are lots of creators who aren't able to produce content on a consistent schedule. In those cases, creators also have the option to charge patrons based on how often they are actually able to publish something.

You're able to set different levels of support starting as low as $1 and going as high as someone is willing to pay. This has the added benefit of allowing patrons to increase their contribution level as your show becomes a bigger part of their life.

Pros: It allows you to budget monthly. Audience growth and commitment can yield more immediate financial impact. Cons: It can be difficult to see results early on. Maintaining patron relations will become a large part of the job.

Crowdfunding's Major Con

Let's talk briefly about donor/patron relations. Remember when I said that I thought crowdfunding was the best monetization option "in almost every way"? We've now reached the "almost" bit . . . You see, in both lump sum and incremental models, you offer additional rewards. Take a look at any Kickstarter/ Indiegogo/Patreon campaign and you'll see what I mean. At the $1 level you get blah, at the $5 level you get such-and-such, at the $10 level, etc. Now, there is nothing inherently wrong with this.

The issue comes in the form of additional work and additional cost. Say every $30 donor/patron gets a T-shirt. Now, along with making new episodes of the show, you also need to get T-shirts made and shipped and deal with any issues that arise. With lump sum campaigns, this usually comes with a *mountain* of work right after the campaign ends. With incremental, the work comes in more manageable chunks, but you have to keep up with it year-round.

With that in mind, I always advise finding rewards based on additional content and access rather than physical goods. It's a lot easier (and cheaper) to record an extra episode just for patrons rather than printing and shipping a hundred bumper stickers. Personally, if I were the patron/donor, I'd pick the additional content any day. You can also do donor-only live streams, a newsletter, or any kind of bonus access like that. It is still additional work, but it is work you are already doing.

More Than Money

Here is a very important factor that a lot of creators either aren't aware of or choose to ignore: donors aren't just giving you money. They are giving you their time, their support, and their trust. I often refer to this as "audience capital," and it is far more valuable than money.

For example, let's say that Todd pledges $1 a month. Now, it doesn't take an economist to tell you that $12 a year isn't a lot of money. However, any creator who thinks that way is doomed to fail. Todd supports you; the actual dollar amount is inconsequential. Todd is there for you and wants you to know that your work matters. He's giving you his money, so he expects you to deliver those delicious new episodes.

So, keep that in mind when you are considering whether you should skip putting an episode out because you don't feel like it. You might be able to skip an episode here and there, but after a while you are going to start burning through your audience capital. Todd might start to wonder why he's supporting a show that hasn't put out an episode in a month. Same goes for those added benefits offered to patrons—if you are supposed to do a monthly livestream, you better do that monthly livestream!

One Weird Option

Before we move on, there is one other option for crowdfunding. I've held off on mentioning it until now because it's kind of weird and doesn't really fit in with the other two models. I think of it as a direct model.

The best example I can think of is to set up a PayPal account and give out the info during the show and on social media.

Let me be clear: in just about every circumstance, I do not advocate for this. First, the lack of overall transparency might scare away donors. Plus, they don't receive any benefit from supporting your show. Finally, at the risk of sounding like a dowager countess, it just isn't done.

All that said, I have used this model before in one very specific case. My friend Hal Lublin and I made a couple of episodes of a show called *Surprisingly Nice*. The idea of the show was to have listeners donate to our PayPal, and then we would donate funds raised to charities of our guests' choosing. I searched around for a better option, but PayPal was the only thing that worked. Even then, it was clunky and the accounting was a job in and of itself.

Crowdfunding Best Practices

- **Put the "fun" in "funding!"** Get people excited to be a part of the fund-raising effort with enticing rewards. Posting videos and other content to push along the campaign never hurts!

- **Talk about it. *A lot.*** No episode of your show should end without you pushing your crowdfunding campaign. Use your social media outlets as well!

- **Don't feel bad asking!** Folks like supporting creators they love. Don't apologize for asking for their support. Be confident and excited!

- **Set reasonable pledge levels.** Don't just offer $1 and $1,000 options—give some increments in between!

- **Don't offer too many levels.** There is absolutely no reason to offer a $1 level and a $2 level and a $3 level and a $4 level and so on. You're creating too much work for yourself. Plus too many options might scare away donors.

- **Budget for rewards.** If you are planning to include physical rewards, make sure you are taking cost into account. It doesn't make a lot of sense to offer a T-shirt to $25 donors if the shirt costs $30 to make and ship.
- **Let folks know where their money is going.** Talk about the better equipment you plan to buy to improve the quality of the show. Talk about how their support makes it easier for you to focus more time and effort on the podcast. Let them know how much their support matters!

Miscellaneous

There are two other, more complicated monetization options that you are probably wondering about, so I wanted to go ahead and address them here.

First, let's talk about **live shows**! Are they an option? Sure they are! However, they can also be extremely complicated to arrange. More often than not, there will also be an up-front cost associated with booking a venue. I would advise holding off on any live show planning until your show has been up and running awhile. If you find you have a dedicated fan base in a fairly centralized area, it may be worth trying. Before you pull the trigger, though, think long and hard about if it is a good move for your show. Not every show translates well to live performance. If you think it works for your podcast, look for smaller, lower-cost venues and keep ticket prices affordable. When deciding on ticket price, the first factor is the cost associated with the show. Say you book a fifty-seat theater and the venue charges a $500 rental fee. Some quick math will inform the lowest price you can charge and not lose money on the show. Once you are ready to sell tickets, talk about it on your show, your social media, and any other avenue you have available to you.

One possibility would be to open for another podcast or comedy show so you can get a feel for how live shows work. If there is a show that regularly performs in your area, or if there is a show coming through your city on tour, reach out and see if the organizers are looking for an opener. There may not be a lot of money in it, but you'll gain invaluable experience!

It also never hurts to ask someone who has been there before. If, in your podcasting journey, you have made connections with other podcasters who tour, I would recommend asking them what they have found that works and what doesn't. It's always better to learn from someone else's mistakes rather than making your own. Also, they may have people who they work with to facilitate tours that they can put you in touch with. They might even be able to connect you with a booking agency. A booking agent will, for a percentage of profits, take on the majority of the work in regard to scheduling the shows, making deals with theaters, and getting tickets on sale. Partnering with a booking agent is a more advanced strategy than a lot of what we have talked about in this book, but if you're going to make touring a real priority, it is worth it.

Another possible place to start would be the increasing number of **podcast festivals and conventions** springing up every year. Even those not focused on podcasting tend to have a couple of live stages. They may not be as financially rewarding as doing it yourself, but being a part of someone else's show is a whole lot easier! Not to mention that most conventions will also offer the chance to sell merch and autographs and/or photo sessions for additional income. Also, there's the added benefit of reaching a new audience that may not know anything about your show but will stop by because they were already at the convention. Start by searching for conventions and festivals in your area. Contact them, tell them about your show, and see if they are looking for performers.

My personal favorite part of attending festivals and conventions is the face-to-face interactions you get to have with your audience. Sitting in your house and talking into a microphone can sometimes feel weird and disconnected. Getting the chance to actually interact with listeners, hear their thoughts on your show, and make a real connection with them can recharge your creativity in a major way. Plus, it's fun!

A couple of notes on submitting your show. Be confident but not boastful. The organizers of the event should be excited to add your show to the lineup. You are not asking them for a favor. This is a mutually beneficial arrangement! They are getting performers, and you are getting to perform. Also, be sure to tell them about your audience. (Size of audience, yes, but also commitment! If your audience is super engaged with the show, let them know!) Don't be discouraged if your show is not accepted on the first try. Many festivals plan their lineups out more than a year in advance. Keep submitting and stay positive!

Finally, you may be wondering about **paywalls**. Just in case you are unfamiliar, a paywall is when people need to pay to listen to the content you create. Well, now that you know what it means, forget about it! Fact is, there's an incalculable amount of free content on the internet. In order to successfully monetize with a paywall, at least one of two conditions needs to be met:

1. Your show features a very famous/incredibly beloved person whom people will happily pay to listen to; and/or
2. Your show is super popular and has a large back catalog that people would be willing to pay a reasonable amount to hear.

If you are just starting out, it's going to be almost im-possible to convince someone to pay to find out if they like your show. That said, there is *one* option you might think about. You could put extended episodes behind a paywall. The sixty-minute episode can be free, but you can make the unedited eighty-minute version available for $0.99—that kind of thing.

However, if you were to go this route, I think it makes more sense to just go the patron route instead of asking for people to pay episode by episode. I tried to do a paywall model once, and it was surprisingly difficult to arrange. Because it is not common for non-network shows to be paywalled, there's not a lot of op-tions for individual creators to use.

Additional Research

I'm going to be honest with you: this has barely scratched the surface of how to be successful at crowdfunding. It has hope-fully given you a place to start, but there are entire books written on the subject. So, if crowdfunding is the path for you, keep researching and preparing! You can do this! I believe in you!

Advertising

WITH GRIFFIN MCELROY

Ah, podcast advertising. Selling out. Shilling for Big Mattress. Hawking website-building platforms to pay the rent. Raking in the *big boys*, by which I mean money.

Shit. You're still reading. Shit, shit, shit.

Okay, look. This is probably the most difficult section I've written so far, and for two very good reasons: first, I'm not really the ad rep for the McElroy Family of Products. I'm more of an *ideas guy*, you know? *Big-picture* stuff. Second, providing any kind of guidance on attracting advertisers to your show when your podcast doesn't even exist yet—well, friend, that's a tough putt.

And yet, advertising is how most professional podcast-makers earn their income. Things like crowdfunding and premium memberships are gaining traction, but advertising is the financial backbone of most of the largest shows out there right now. The Interactive Advertising Bureau estimates that podcasting revenue will exceed $1 billion by 2021. Maybe some of that could be yours! (Most of that will be ours. Do *not* front. We're happy to have you as our literary pupil, but if you come for the throne, you'd better come correct.)

Here's where things get complicated. There are a lot of

different ways to get ads on your show. There are a lot of different ways to *surface* those ads. There are a lot of different variables that add up to what advertisers are looking for in a partner podcast. There are a lot of different benefits *you* might be able to offer to make your show attractive to advertisers.

There isn't a single path to luring in advertisers, so you probably aren't going to come out of this section with an especially firm business plan. Instead, I'll lay out how it works *most of the time* and give a few tips on what to expect if you decide to go in this particularly fungible direction.

Also, it's worth noting right here at the top: **if your show doesn't exist yet or is still in its infancy, you're not going to have any advertisers for a while**. Most ad agencies aren't going to talk to you until your show starts bringing in some thousand downloads a month. If you want to skip ahead and return to this chapter after you become a big, big star, I won't be offended.

How Podcast Advertising Works

On the micro scale, podcast advertising is when a company pays nerds in order to get them to talk about its artisanal mouthwash *or whatever.*

Now, let's zoom out. Who arranged for this transaction

between the nerds and the mouthwash company? Almost certainly not the nerds themselves. More than likely a third party representing the podcast arranged the deal, negotiating a fair price based on any number of measurements of the show's listenership.

For a lot of shows, that means an **ad agency**. Ad agencies (or ad networks) are the middlemen of the podcast advertising game—though I don't use that term as a pejorative. Most ad agencies represent a bunch of shows and have relationships with a bunch of advertisers. When a company wants to advertise a product, an ad agency can find the show that's the exact right fit and facilitate the sale *way* more easily than, say, myself, a business-averse dipshit.

When I say "right fit," I'm describing the biggest strength of podcasts as an advertising platform and the fuel for the outrageous growth in advertiser spending on podcasts over the last few years. There are a *lot* of shows out there about nearly every conceivable topic. A Super Bowl commercial probably isn't going to achieve a lot of market penetration for your artisanal mouthwash company, but a three-minute spot on *Gargle Boys: The Mouthwash Enthusiast Podcast*? That's an absolute slam dunk.

So: the ad agency arranges a deal between Fancylad Mouthwash™ and *Gargle Boys* and takes a portion of the ad revenue in exchange. But how much revenue did it bring in in the first place? That number changes based on an infinite array of variables, but as a general rule of thumb:

- The more listeners your show has
- The more engaged those listeners are with your show
- The more endemic your show is for the product being advertised (see: *Gargle Boys*)
- The more amenable your show is to the advertiser's wishes

The more money you're going to pull in for any given ad sale

Tracking listeners is easy enough: most podcast hosting platforms can generate download reports by time period or region, and that's info that any advertiser is going to want.

On the Subject of Download Counts

How many downloads should your podcast achieve before you start seeking advertising representation? That's a good, largely unanswerable question. It's kind of a moving target! If you look around at the different platforms that exist today, most have a minimum before you can apply for them. As a point of reference, if you use Libsyn as your host, it can sell ads for you—once your show reaches five thousand downloads in the United States per month. Midroll, one of the largest podcast ad reps, suggests thirty thousand downloads per episode for eligibility. Note that those caps usually only apply to traditional ad agencies—more peer-to-peer stuff like Anchor typically doesn't have a bar to clear.

Tracking podcast engagement isn't as clear-cut as tracking downloads. Instead of discovering how many people like your show, you're trying to figure out *how much* they like your show. Some hosting services can provide data on how much of each episode folks listen to on average, which is certainly useful. For most other cases, audience engagement is measured in likes, reviews, and subscriptions. If you've got a favorable ratio of listeners to subscribers, you're in good shape.

How related your show's subject is to the advertisement itself is fairly self-explanatory. Mouthwash companies will pay a premium to have the hosts of *Gargle Boys* read their copy, provided that the eponymous Gargle Boys are okay with such a flagrant breach of mouthwash enthusiast ethical standards.

I'm goofing, of course, but endemic advertising is something you should take seriously just in case it's a bridge you're ever faced with crossing. Is it possible (or even important) for your show to remain completely objective if you've been paid to advertise something related to the subject matter of the show? There are a few schools of thought on this, but we've always been fairly conservative when approached by endemic advertisers. When in doubt, lean on the old adage: the appearance of impropriety is as bad as impropriety itself.

Which brings us to our last point: What are you willing to offer, content-wise, to the advertisers themselves?

There are three types of traditional podcast ads, differentiated by where they land in the show's running time. **Pre-roll** ads run before the podcast and are usually the shortest of the bunch, running around fifteen to thirty seconds. **Mid-roll** ads are the most common, usually run for longer, and are interspersed throughout the main body of an episode. **Post-roll** ads are placed at the very end of an episode and are often paired with pre-roll ads to serve as bookends.

There's a ton of different philosophies and value propositions for these three types of ads, but the traditional breakdown is that post-roll ads are the least valued, as folks are more likely to turn off the show before they run, while pre-roll and mid-roll ads are more sought after.

Pre-roll ads can, on paper, guarantee a listener hears the advertisement, as it leads into the rest of the show. On the other hand, it's arguably the most skippable advertisement; it's not difficult for a listener to press Play, hear an ad start, then move their thumb over to the Fast-Forward button in one swift motion. Mid-roll ads are less likely to get skipped in this method, provided they don't overstay their welcome.

Another, more extreme advertising deal may entail you creating a **sponsored episode**, which is by far the most lucrative arrangement you can snag. It is also the most difficult needle to thread, content-wise. To make an episode where you vociferously endorse a product while still remaining entertaining and listenable is no small feat.

At the time of this writing, we've done two sponsored episodes of *My Brother, My Brother and Me*. One was a Totino's Pizza Roll–fueled fever dream, and the other was a *profoundly quiet* ASMR episode for Casper mattresses. We've been approached to do others but couldn't think of ways to make them enjoyable to record and listen to—those two lent themselves to concepts we thought we could have fun with, so we took them on.

And, on that note, the other thing you can negotiate is the copy you'll be asked to read as part of the deal. A good ad agency or network won't force you into any kind of endorsement that you're not comfortable with, but the harder you're willing to go—reading a scripted call to action, guaranteeing a discussion of personal experience with the product, etc.—the more lucrative a deal your agency will be able to snag.

Dynamic Ad Insertion

This sounds like a really fancy term, but it's fairly basic. In the early years of podcasting, hosts would either read ads or download them from a sponsor and edit them into their show. Some shows still do; some always will. No matter when someone downloads an episode, they'll always hear the same ads. This is bad for the podcaster, because you only get paid to put an ad in once, and no matter how popular an episode gets, you don't get more cash.

With dynamic ad insertion, ads aren't edited into the show from the beginning, they're automatically slipped in at the moment the listener downloads the episode. This means that even if a listener gets a three-year-old episode, they will still hear a new ad. This is good because you can earn revenue on older episodes, but the trade-off is that it's harder to fold ads naturally into the context of the show. It's a little more stilted.

The other negative, from a listener's point of view, is that if they're binging a show, they could end up hearing the same ad a *lot* of times. I listened to the entirety of *Reply All* in two weeks and can still recite word for word the ad copy for the Netflix movie being advertised.

What All This Means for Your New Show

The traditional advertising model isn't necessarily a great fit for a podcast that's just starting out and seeking its first dozen die-hard fans to build a community out of. Advertising is, inherently, when companies pay to get a message out to lots of people. If your show doesn't reach lots of people, you're probably not going to get in on the advertising game at the moment.

Unless you sign up with a hosting platform like Anchor, which, if you opt into advertising, matches you with potential advertisers directly through the app. You can see how much said ad will pay, check out the copy and instructions, record and plop it into an episode with relative ease, and then track how much you've earned, which pays out whenever you want. It's designed with the hobbyist in mind, and if you're eager to start making (some) money earlyish in the lifespan of your show, it's worth considering.

That doesn't mean your show can't be a lucrative exercise during its early days! Crowdfunding platforms are way more conducive for supporting a smaller show. And, once your show hits that magic, indefinable threshold, you can find an ad network you're comfortable with and start slinging mouthwash!

If advertising does manage to become a consideration for your show, make sure you find ways to keep your content *relatively* entertaining for your listeners and not, you know, dry as a popcorn fart. We've handled ads on *My Brother, My Brother and Me* with the same general tone as the rest of the show, which is, you know, that twisted *South Park* humor. Some of our most memorable bits have come out of those ad spots, which is good not only because we didn't bore our audience to tears, but also because *damn*, advertisers like when folks still talk about those ad bits.

Which brings me to my last tip with regard to advertising: figure out what you're willing to give away, how hard in the paint you're willing to go when talking about goods and services, and then stick to it. It's a really tricky needle to thread, and having a good, trustworthy ad agency in your corner makes it immeasurably easier.

Oh, and once you're getting that mattress money and trying to decide which turbo yacht you want to buy first: you can't go wrong with a Bertram 61. The sportfishing deck, it's just . . . you gotta ride it to believe it. Beautiful.

Outroduction
with Griffin McElroy

And with that, you have officially wrung us dry, collecting all of our experiential wisdom juices to the brim of your mind-cup.

Okay, that's probably not entirely accurate. There are likely some bits of podcasting errata that we didn't think would be helpful writ large. For example, your body is about to become a podcasting machine, so how can you *physiologically* optimize your recording sessions? (Answer: **CARBOLOAD**.)

Hopefully, by this point, you understand enough of the basics to get started. We've read enough manuals of this sort to know that *doing* the thing is an entirely different prospect from *reading about doing* the thing. There may be a fair number of you who close this well-meaning tome, never to act on its lessons.

That's fine! We'll always cherish the time we've spent together. How about we meet back here in this same spot in ten years, both wearing red carnations?

For the rest of you, you enterprising *casters of pod*, you're hypothetically ready to take the next steps into the arena. What are those steps, you ask?

Really? Like, we just spent a whole honest-to-God book laying out a detailed list of considerations to ponder as you get started in podcasting. What do you want now, a checklist? A TL;DR? Some kind of podcasting vision board? *Pearls before swine*, we say!

Oh, you just want to know what to do *first?* Like, as soon as you finish reading, when you're filled with creativity and drive, and you're excited to get started immediately? There's actually an easy answer for that, and hopefully, in providing that answer, we'll be able to squeeze in one more dank wisdom nug right here in the epilogue:

Do anything.

That's it. You've maybe already done some stuff. Perhaps you've already found a serviceable microphone and you've familiarized yourself with the DAW of your choosing. Maybe you've whipped up a rundown with your new cohosts and hired a talented artist friend to draw up some album art. Or maybe you haven't done anything at all! That's fine too.

The point is this: the only thing you need to do to make a

podcast is *make a podcast*. When writing this book, that's the end goal we tried to stay focused on. We've included all the podcast-related things we've thought about during our decade or so in the biz, but the second you find yourself endlessly deliberating over one of the topics we've covered, you have our explicit permission to *jettison that shit*.

Don't let yourself get mired into setting up a professional-grade recording studio before you've even recorded your pilot. Don't put off workshopping ideas with your pals until you've devised a lucrative marketing plan. If you notice that something is serving as a roadblock to actually recording the thing, just skip it! Get the cheap mic! Dive in unprepared! If you wait until you're sure you're ready to make the best version of that thing, you're never going to make anything.

Experience will be a far more capable teacher than this book could ever be. As some football coach probably said one time: failure is weakness leaving the body. Or something.

If you find yourself truly stuck in a rut, unable to follow through on this new pursuit, we've got an exercise for you. This is something you can do *right now*, if you want. Just keep the book propped up on the table with one hand as you go, because—and we should have mentioned this earlier—every time you close this book, our consciousness is banished back into the Bibliorealm. What's that like? Well, it's a kind of death, so, yeah, *keep it cracked*, eh?

Sit down at your computer. (Not at your computer? Get your phone.) Open up a voice recorder app. Most OSes come with one. Windows has one simply called Voice Recorder. On Mac, try Voice Memos. On Linux . . . man, I don't know. Type in the unnecessarily complex string of code required to access some kind of audio-recording software, fuckin' Mr. Robot.

Your computer probably has some kind of built-in microphone. (Your phone *for sure* has one, because if not—hey, bud? You sure that's a phone?) If it doesn't, you probably have *something* nearby capable of interpreting sound as computer data. Maybe a webcam, or a gaming headset, or some earbuds? Plug that in. Now, press Record.

And start talking. Really. About whatever. What's the thing you spend most of your day thinking about? What's something you wish more people knew about you? What's the story you tell folks when everyone's telling stories and you want to really just slam-dunk everyone else's story right into the garbage can? What are you worried about? What kind of stuff do you think about to help you deal with the stuff you're worried about?

Okay, now *wrap it up*. Don't overstay your welcome. Save something for next time.

And press Stop.

And just like that, you've recorded . . .

Oh shit, save! Oh my God, always, *always* save. I don't know if we've mentioned that enough in this book yet. It's, like, the *most* important thing.

Did you save? Okay. Great.

And just like that, you've recorded an episode of a podcast. Don't get caught up in the technicalities. Don't freeze up because you weren't as funny or clever or charming as you'd hoped. You *did* it. You made the thing. *That's* the baseline. That's the thing you'll be able to make better with the stuff you've hopefully taken away from this book.

Next time you record something, try to fix a few things that you didn't quite nail the first time around. Maybe try recording in a DAW, where you can drop some music over the beginning and end of the track. If you didn't quite nail the pacing, focus on that this time around. You're not going to perfect the craft on your second attempt either. Just try again, and fix something, and try again, and think of ways to improve, and try again . . . and so on.

With all that in mind: Yes, friend, **podcasting is easy**. Considering the full spectrum of the comparative difficulty of potential human endeavors, clicking Record, talking for a while, and then clicking Stop ranks very, *very* low. But making something worth listening to, something people will remember, something you'll find creative satisfaction in, can be as challenging and time consuming as you want it to be.

Make *something*, and then make it better. That's not just how we learned to competently make podcasts we're proud of; it's how *anyone* learns how to do *anything*. Just go record something—right now, if you're able—and *then* think about how to internalize what you've learned from this book. And if you need a refresher, feel free to grab it off the bookshelf, dust it off, and give it another whirl.

Until then, we'll be twirling, twirling eternally, in the perfect nothingness of the Bibliorealm. *Farewell.*

You Honestly Want More McElroy Content?

Well, there's plenty of it, but we warn you, you'll want to pace yourselves—and be sure to hydrate. (Also skip the first 150 episodes or so of *MBMBaM* for good measure. We weren't kidding, the early ones are rough to listen to.)

If it's podcasts you're after, *MBMBaM*, *Sawbones*, *Shmanners*, *Wonderful!*, *The Besties*, and *Still Buffering* come out weekly. *The Adventure Zone* and *The Empty Bowl* come out every other week, and *Til Death Do Us Blart* comes out annually on American Thanksgiving. You can subscribe to any of our shows in the podcatcher of your choice, save for *The Besties*, which is a free Spotify exclusive show.

If television is more your thing, you can watch all six episodes of the *My Brother, My Brother and Me* show, made for

Seeso, available for purchase wherever ill-fated TV shows are found. We're also developing an animated version of *The Adventure Zone* for NBC's Peacock, but you'll have to wait for that one.

We should have opened with this, but your simplest option is to go to our website, http://www.TheMcElroy.Family. It's where you'll find links to all the latest episodes of our shows in addition to, well, everything else we do. We share new episodes of our video series like *Monster Factory* and *Things I Bought at Sheetz*, information about upcoming live shows, new merch each month, updates on our other projects (there's a TAZ board game!), and more. You can even find information about our other books! Yes, we've written others—we know, we can't believe it either.

However you decide to dive into the rich and strange world of content we've created over the last decade, we thank you. Seriously, it's a wildly unexpected thing to get to make a living in this manner, and it's thanks to folks like you who encounter something we've made and decide, against all reason, that you'd like to check out more. We're forever in your debt.

Acknowledgments

As we have established at length, we are simple people of limited objective value, so the fact that this book exists at all is a tribute to the kind people that cared enough to help it exist.

We owe our editor, Amy Baker, and our literary agent, Jodi Reamer, an immense debt for their work in helping this book come together, as well as Sarah McKay for her design work that makes it such a delight to look at. Everyone at Harper Perennial was a delight and a treasure, in fact.

We're so thankful to Sydnee, Teresa, and Rachel McElroy for lending us not only their talent and insight, but also their patience and support every day of our lives.

Joel Begleiter had nothing to do with this book, but he's

been a fierce, loyal advocate for us for years, so he made it into the acknowledgments too. Ditto to Jesse Thorn who took a chance on us and changed our lives.

The small yet scrappy team behind the McElroy family, Sarah Davis, Sarah McKay (doubly acknowledged now), Alice Flanders, Paul Sabourin, Alexx Rouse, and Alex Turner work harder than us and get less of the credit, and we hope they never wise up and ditch us. Super duper special thanks to our hero and manager, Amanda Freberg, the best boss we could have hoped for.

Lastly, we would like to thank our mom and dad, Leslie and Clint McElroy, for getting it in our heads that we could make something worth listening to or reading in the first place. We don't know how we could ever repay them for the years of food, shelter, and love, but we figure including them in our acknowledgments gets us pretty close to square.

Index

Adventure Zone, The
  music on, 145
  release schedule, 34
  social media accounts,
      188–89
  software tools, 75, 84–85
  statistics, 161
  structure of, 23, 24
advertising
  ad agencies and networks,
      161–62, 222, 223, 225,
      227, 230
  ad copy, 161, 227–28
  download counts, 222,
      224–25
  dynamic ad insertion, 161,
      227–28
  endemic, 225–26
  hosting services and, 161–62
  new shows and, 229–30
  in show structure, 31–32
  sponsored episodes, 226–27
  tracking engagement for,
      224–25
  types of ads, 226
ambient noise, 66, 89–91, 92,
    119–20

analytics, 160–61, 168, 225
Anchor, 160, 163, 225, 229
Anna Faris Is Unqualified, 2
Apple Podcasts, 165, 166–70,
    171–73
art, 189–93, 205, 207
attention and focus, 68, 101–3,
    109
Audacity, 75–80, 82, 85, 86
audience capital, 213–14
audience/listeners
  appreciating, 173–75
  building, 4, 6, 21, 201
  competing for time/
      attention of, 195
  engagement tracking, 225
  expectations and listening
      habits of, 24, 31,
      33–34, 52
  niche, 8
  recording for, 18, 19, 20,
      103–5
  respecting, 28, 131–32,
      184–85
  statistics on, 9, 26–27,
      160–61
  topic ideas from, 41, 194

audience/listeners,
     communicating with
 by email, 175–79
 feedback, 90, 148–56, 197–98
 at listening parties, 181–82
 meeting in-person, 182–84,
     218–19
 on social media, 179–81,
     193–94, 196–97
 from voicemail, 181
audio interfaces, 64–65
audio processing tools, 84
audio quality
 hardware and, 58, 63–64,
     65, 66, 69
 listener feedback on, 90
 software and, 83–84

background noise, 66, 89–91,
     92, 119–20
Batt, Tim, 10
Besties, The, 13–14
binaural recording pattern, 63
binge-listening, 4, 15, 122
Black, Brent, 11, 18
bloopers, 129
Blue Yeti mic, 63–64
booking agents, 218

cable connections, 62–65, 66,
     68–69, 70
CAD E100S microphones, 66

cardioid recording pattern, 60,
     63
Carnegie, Dale, 174–75
Carolla, Adam, 159, 162
categories, 166, 171–73
ccMixter, 140
chart rankings, 171–72
"Chocolate Rain" (Zonday),
     105
CleanFeed, 83, 84
cohosts
 actively listening to, 115–19
 dynamic/chemistry with,
     17–18, 35, 46, 101, 102
 early decisions about,
     14–20
 relationships with, 115, 120
 researching and, 35, 42, 46,
     48, 52–53
 roles of, 19, 52, 53–54
 vs. rotating guests, 15–16,
     20–22
 scheduling with, 32
competitive research, 8–10,
     191–92
concept, finding and pitching,
     2–3
condenser mics, 59
contributions, listener, 163
conventions, 183, 218–19
copyrighted music, 136–37,
     138, 145–47

cough button, 70
Creative Commons, 139–40
cross-fades, 133
cross-promotion, 163
cross-referencing, 51
crowdfunding
    audience capital and,
        213–14
    best practices for, 215–16
    direct model for, 214–15
    incremental *vs.* lump sum,
        209–12
    pros and cons of, 209,
        212–13, 229–30
    rewards, 212–13, 215, 216
    through live shows, 216–18
    through paywalls, 219–20

DAWs (digital audio
    workstations)
    Audacity, 75–80, 82, 85, 86
    choosing, 74–77
    editing with, 77, 131, 133,
        145
    making music with, 84–85,
        140
    recording with, 77, 86, 135
DFTBA, 204
differentiating yourself, 10–11
Discord, 72, 83
distractions, avoiding, 101–2
dog training clicker, 70, 129

donations, 163
download counts, 161, 222,
    224–25
dynamic ad insertion, 161,
    227–28
dynamic mics, 58–59

eating and drinking, 71–72,
    107–8
editing
    background noise, 119–20
    dog training clicker for, 70,
        129
    fades and transitions, 133,
        142, 144–45
    headphones for, 68
    "in the moment," 130
    in multiple passes, 128–34
    off-mic bits and, 120,
        122–23, 129
    recording mindset and,
        119–21, 126–27
    removing evidence of,
        132–33
    saving raw file, 126
    silent pauses for, 121, 129
    using DAWs for, 77, 131,
        133, 145
electrical tape, multicolored,
    69–70
email, 175–79
embedded episodes, 163

Empty Bowl, The, 7, 82, 92, 100
endemic advertising, 225–26
energy, 109–10, 122
engagement, tracking, 224–25
Enlow, Courtney, 11, 16, 18
expertise, 10–11, 37, 39–40,
    53, 99
extended episodes, 220

Facebook, 180, 186, 196–97
fact-checking, 39, 51, 52
fades, 133, 142, 145
fair use, 145–47
fan pages, 196–97
feedback from listeners, 90,
    148–56, 197–98
festivals, 218–19
figure 8 recording pattern, 61,
    63
filler words, editing, 133–34
focus and attention, 68, 101–3,
    109
Free Music Archive, 140
friction, 31, 141

GarageBand, 85
genre, 37
goal/mission, 6–8, 36–40, 131
GoFundMe, 209, 210
Goubert, Dan, 7
guests, 15–16, 19, 20–22
*Guys We F****d*, 12, 162

Hardcore History, 28
headphones, 67–69, 142
headspace, 100–101
hosting services, 158–64,
    165–66
humor, 112–13
hypercardioid recording
    pattern, 60

ID3 Editor app, 85
idea meat, 30
improv shows, 112
Indiegogo, 209, 210
intentional noise, 92
internet, shitty behavior and,
    178–79
internet browsers, 74, 85
interrupting with intention, 118
intro, creating, 29
"(It's a) Departure" (Long
    Winters), 143
iTunes, 169

Jordan, Jesse, Go!, 32

Kickstarter, 209, 210
Kingkiller Chronicle series
    (Rothfuss), 103

lapel mics, 66
lavalier (lapel) mics, 66
Levelator app, 84

Libsyn, 26, 159, 162, 163–64, 168, 224
listener friction, 31
listeners. *See* audience/listeners
listening, 115–19, 132
listening platforms. *See* podcast platforms
Logic Pro X app, 84–85
logos, 191, 192–93
Long Winters, 143
Lublin, Hal, 215

Machinimasound, 138
marketing and promotion. *See also* audience/listeners, communicating with; social media
  art and logo for, 189–93
  discoverability in, 170–73
  merchandise and, 201
  strategy for, 184–85
  submitting to podcast platforms, 165–70
Maron, Marc, 162
McElroy Brothers Will Be in "Trolls 2," The, 3
McElroy Brothers Will Be in "Trolls World Tour," The, 131
meetups with listeners, 182–83

Megaphone, 162
Memory Palace, The, 27–28
merchandise, selling, 200–208, 218
metadata, 85, 166, 169
microphones
  cable connections, 62–67
  cost of, 63, 65–66
  multiple, 62, 64
  muting, 70
  recording patterns, 59–61, 95
  types of, 58–59, 66
  windscreens and soundproofing for, 69, 95, 106
microphone stands, 67
mic technique, 105–6
mid-roll ads, 226
mistakes, acknowledging, 52–53
mixing, 144
money, making, 4. *See also* advertising; contributions; crowdfunding; merchandise, selling
mono recording, 80–81
Montgomery, Guy, 10
mood, 100–101
music
  background, 144
  choosing, 29, 141–43

music (*cont.*)
Creative Commons, 139–40
fades and transitions, 142, 144–45
fair use, 145–47
interstitial, 143, 145
intro and outro, 143
making your own, 84–85, 140
mixing, 144
sourcing, 136–40, 145
theme songs, 141–43
Musicbed, 138
My Brother, My Brother and Me
advertising, 227, 230
chart rankings, 172
cohosts on, 16
editing process used for, 82, 132
hosting services used for, 159, 161
interruptions with intention, 118
listener communication, 177, 181–82
merchandise for, 200–201, 208
microphones used for, 58
music on, 143
naming of, 13
pitch for, 3

recording, 90, 93–94, 111, 112–13, 132
release schedule for, 34
software used for, 82
statistics, 161
structure of, 22–23, 30
My Favorite Murder, 207

name, picking, 11–14, 188–89
99% Invisible, 10
"no, buting," 114–15
noise
ambient, 89–91, 119–20
intentional, 92
sound waves and, 93–96
Nox, 162

obsessions, 6–8
off-mic, 120, 122–23, 129
omnidirectional recording pattern, 60–61, 63
outro, creating, 29–30, 123
outtakes, 129

Patreon, 211
patron-based models, 211–13
PayPal, 214
performing, 109–10
persona, 109–10
phantom power, 59
phone, avoiding distraction of, 101, 102

physical listening, 116–17
pitch, 2–3
plosives, 69, 106
Pocket Casts, 165, 167
podcasting
    accepting your limitations,
        127–28
    ad revenue from, 221
    art of, 99
    "first steps," 232–36
    interactivity of, 194
podcast listening
    audience habits and
        expectations, 24,
        26–27, 31, 33–34, 52
    binging, 4, 15, 122
    episode length and, 26–27
podcast platforms
    adding your show to, 165–70
    advertising with, 224–25
    hosting statistics on, 161
    logo specifications for, 191
    vs. podcast hosts, 165–66
    search and findability on,
        172–73
podcatchers. See podcast
    platforms
polar patterns. See recording
    patterns
Positiviteeny!, 12
postproduction. See also editing;
    marketing and promotion

release schedule and time
    budgeted for, 32
uploading, 158, 159, 160,
    165, 166
post-roll ads, 226
preproduction. See cohosts;
    research; show structure;
    topics
pre-roll ads, 226

raw files, saving, 126, 234–35
REAPER digital audio
    workstation, 75
recording
    audience and, 18, 19, 20,
        103–5
    being funny, 112–13
    brainwork during, 112,
        116–17
    eating and drinking during,
        71–72, 107–8
    editing mindset for, 119–21
    ending the episode, 121–23
    headspace/mood during,
        100–101, 120
    improv shows, 112
    listening during, 115–19
    mic technique for, 105–6
    in mono vs. stereo, 80–81,
        82
    performing during, 109–10
    pushing crowdfunding, 215

recording (*cont.*)

    remotely, 19–20, 70, 72–73, 83, 117

    in same room, 19–20

    speaking cues during, 117–18

    standing *vs.* sitting during, 97

    staying focused during, 68, 101–3, 109

    topic choice for, 111–12

    using DAWs for, 77, 79–82

    "yes, anding," 113–15

recording environment, 70, 87–88, 94–98

recording patterns, 59–61, 62, 63, 106

Reddit, 196

release schedules, 32–35

research

    accuracy and, 39, 43, 51, 52

    cohost dynamic and, 42, 46, 48, 52–53

    digging deeper, 43–44

    expertise and, 37, 39–40, 53

    finding information, 43–46

    finding the story, 47–50

    finding topics, 9–10, 41–43

    keeping records of, 51–52

    learning the topic, 46, 48

    owning mistakes, 52–53

    paring down, 46, 48–49, 52–53

    show goal/purpose and, 36–40, 42, 49

    sources for, 43–45, 51–52

    starting with summary articles, 43

    topic breadth and, 39, 42

    of your competition, 8–10, 191–92

ribbon mics, 59

roadblocks, skipping, 233

ropes, swinging on, 112, 114

Rose Buddies, 40

Rothfuss, Patrick, 103

RSS feed, 159, 164, 166, 168

Satellite Dish, 92

saving files, 126, 234–35

Sawbones: A Marital Tour of Misguided Medicine

    editing, 132

    expertise and, 10–11

    genre of, 37

    merchandise, 207

    mission of, 37

    naming of, 3

    research for, 36–37, 38, 43–44

    structure of, 30–31

scheduling, 19–20, 32–35

scripted *vs.* nonscripted
formats, 23–25, 45–46
search, on-platform, 172
Shmanners
cohost roles in, 16, 53–54
episode length, 122
listener expectations for,
49
research for, 37, 38, 44, 49
topic criteria for, 111
shotgun (figure 8) recording
pattern, 61, 63
show name, picking, 11–14,
188–89
show structure
advertising breaks, 31–32
benefits of planning, 24, 31
length of, 23, 25–28, 122
morning release target,
34–35
recording trial episode, 35
release schedule, 32–35
scripted *vs.* nonscripted,
23–25, 45–46
segments, 29–35
transitions, 30–31, 32
troubleshooting, 32–35
tweaking, 22–23, 25, 31
Shure SM58 microphone, 65
silence, 116, 118, 121, 129,
134
single-voice formats, 14–15

sitting *vs.* standing, 97
Skype, 72, 83
Slack, 83
social media
communicating with
listeners on, 179–81,
193–94, 196–97
crowdfunding through, 215
feedback from, 197–98
keepin' it classy on, 180–81,
198
logo specifications for,
192–93
online presence for, 188,
194
promoting episode releases,
193, 194
risks of, 180–81
scope of, 187–88
show name and, 13,
188–89
sound bleed, 68
soundboards, 64
sound effects, 82, 92
sound interfaces, 64–65
sound patterns, 59–61, 62, 63
soundproofing, 69, 87, 94–96,
106
sound waves, 93–96
speaking cues, 117–18
splitters, 68–69
sponsored episodes, 227

Spotify, 165, 167, 170

standing *vs.* sitting, 97

statistics, 160–61, 168. *See also* download counts

stereo recording, 81, 82

Stop Podcasting Yourself, 12–13

stories

    differentiating yourself with, 10

    episode length and, 23

    finding and researching, 45, 46, 47–50

    scripted *vs.* nonscripted, 23–24, 45–46

    telling, 109

subscriptions, 33–34, 225

supercardioid recording pattern, 60

Surprisingly Nice, 215

Survivor-themed shows, 9–10

taglines, 123, 207

theme songs, 141–43

Thurston, Howard, 174–75

topics

    breadth/depth of, 33, 39, 42

    criteria for, 111

    differentiating from competitors, 10

    expertise and, 10–11, 37, 39–40, 53

    finding stories within, 47–50

    gauging your interest in, 6–8, 38, 44–45, 53, 111–12

    listener suggestions for, 41, 194

    researching, 9–10, 39, 41–43, 46, 48

    viewing through different lenses, 11

    when to abandon, 31, 42–43, 48

transitions, 30–31, 32, 142, 144–45

Trends Like These, 11, 16, 18

trial episode, recording, 35

trolls, responding to, 177–79

T-shirts, selling, 199–205

Twitter, 180–81, 187, 194

USB connections, 62, 63, 64

video clips, 195

voicemail, 181–82

VoIP (Voice over Internet Protocol) apps, 72–73, 74, 83–84

Walch, Rob, 26

water, 107–8

websites, 162, 197
Wikipedia, 43
windscreens, 69, 106
WNYC, 162
Wonderful!, 25, 40, 50, 74–75
Worst Idea of All Time, The,
    10
WTF, 162

XLR connections, 62, 63, 64,
    66

"yes, anding," 113–15
YouTube, 195

Zonday, Tay, 105
Zoom, 65, 72

About the Authors

Justin, Travis, and Griffin McElroy are podcasters and authors from Huntington, West Virginia. They are the creators of the *My Brother, My Brother and Me* podcast and television show, and along with their father Clint McElroy, the podcast and #1 *New York Times* bestselling graphic novel series *The Adventure Zone*. With their wives and friends they make other podcasts, including *Sawbones* (also a *New York Times* bestselling book); *Shmanners*; and *Wonderful!*. They are also featured in the Dreamworks motion picture *Trolls World Tour* (well, their voices are, you know, it's a cartoon).

Justin still lives in Huntington, West Virginia; Travis lives in Cincinnati, Ohio; and Griffin lives in Austin, Texas.